Letters to Students

Letters to Students

What It Means to Be a College Graduate

Dr. Drew Bogner and Dr. Robert A. Scott

ROWMAN & LITTLEFIELD
Lanham • Boulder • New York • London

Published by Rowman & Littlefield
An imprint of The Rowman & Littlefield Publishing Group, Inc.
4501 Forbes Boulevard, Suite 200, Lanham, Maryland 20706
www.rowman.com

86-90 Paul Street, London EC2A 4NE

Copyright © 2024 by Drew Bogner and Robert Allyn Scott

All rights reserved. No part of this book may be reproduced in any form or by any electronic or mechanical means, including information storage and retrieval systems, without written permission from the publisher, except by a reviewer who may quote passages in a review.

British Library Cataloguing in Publication Information Available

Library of Congress Cataloging-in-Publication Data

Names: Bogner, Drew, 1957- author. | Scott, Robert A. (Robert Allyn), 1939- author.
Title: Letters to students : what it means to be a college graduate / Drew Bogner and Robert Allyn Scott.
Description: Lanham : Rowman & Littlefield Publishers, [2024]
Identifiers: LCCN 2024011241 (print) | LCCN 2024011242 (ebook) | ISBN 9781475873726 (cloth) | ISBN 9781475873733 (paperback) | ISBN 9781475873740 (ebook)
Subjects: LCSH: Motivation in education. | College graduates--Life skills guides. | College students--Social conditions. | College student orientation. | Mentoring in education.
Classification: LCC LB1065 .B63 2024 (print) | LCC LB1065 (ebook) | DDC 370.15/4--dc23/eng/20240314
LC record available at https://lccn.loc.gov/2024011241
LC ebook record available at https://lccn.loc.gov/2024011242

We do not achieve success in life or in college without the assistance and inspiration of those few select individuals who serve as mentors and advisors. This book is dedicated to three remarkable individuals who served in that capacity for me during periods of transition and growth. Dr. Surendra Singh and S. Tarcisia Roths were my two advisors during my undergraduate years at Kansas Newman College, now Newman University, Dr. Singh for my biology and premed major and Dr. Roths for my history major. Dr. Singh taught me, by his quiet and measured passion and ethical standards, to live a life of principle. Sister Tarcisia, in addition to being an academic advisor, was also my spiritual advisor and taught me how to live a life of purpose. Eventually I returned to Newman to teach alongside Surendra and eventually became his "boss," serving as the chief academic officer for S. Tarcisia during her nine years as president.

My third and most important mentor has always been my wife, Karen. She was my editor, counselor, and advisor for those 30 years that I served as vice president and president. Beginning with my decision to leave medical school and pursue a career in higher education, Karen taught me how to listen to myself and summon the courage to live a life of personal conviction and passion.

—Dr. Drew Bogner

For a book about navigating college successfully, I can think of no better dedication than to acknowledge the help of my high school biology teacher turned college counselor and my Bucknell English professor and advisor. If it weren't for the first, Joe Leone, I might not have gone to college. If it weren't for the second, Dr. Mildred Martin, I might not have stayed. I am grateful to them and have tried to serve students as they served me.

I also dedicate this book to my wife, Carole Artigiani, founder of Global Kids (globalkids.org), the highly acclaimed youth development organization in NYC and Washington, DC. I have learned a thing or two about young people from her over the years.

—Dr. Robert A. Scott

Contents

Chapter Summaries   xi

Foreword   xix
   Carla Deazle, PhD

Acknowledgments   xxi

Preface   xxiii

Introduction to Students and Graduates   xxix
   Dr. Drew Bogner and Dr. Robert A. Scott

Chapter 1: Living a Life of Success   1
   Dr. Drew Bogner, president emeritus, Molloy University

Chapter 2: Getting the Most out of College   7
   Dr. Robert A. Scott, president emeritus, Adelphi University

Chapter 3: Finding and Using Your Voice   13
   Dr. Robert A. Scott, president emeritus, Adelphi University

Chapter 4: Don't Listen   19
   Dr. Drew Bogner, president emeritus, Molloy University

Chapter 5: What Are the Liberal Arts, Anyway?   23
   Dr. Robert A. Scott, president emeritus, Adelphi University

Chapter 6: Syllabus for Your Life   27
   Dr. Drew Bogner, president emeritus, Molloy University

Chapter 7: How Do We Know What We Think We Know?   31
   Dr. Robert A. Scott. president emeritus, Adelphi University

Chapter 8: Let Your Life Speak 35
Dr. Drew Bogner, president emeritus, Molloy University

Chapter 9: How Should I Serve Others? 39
Dr. Robert A. Scott, president emeritus, Adelphi University

Chapter 10: Who Do You Want to Be? 43
Dr. Robert A. Scott, president emeritus, Adelphi University

Chapter 11: Trust Yourself 47
Dr. Robert A. Scott, president emeritus, Adelphi University

Chapter 12: Choices and Decisions 51
Dr. Drew Bogner, president emeritus, Molloy University

Chapter 13: Why Diversity Matters 55
Dr. Robert A. Scott, president emeritus, Adelphi University

Chapter 14: What You Say Matters 59
Dr. Drew Bogner, president emeritus, Molloy University

Chapter 15: Being an Effective Leader 63
Dr. Drew Bogner, president emeritus, Molloy University

Chapter 16: Developing Leadership Skills 69
Dr. Robert A. Scott, president emeritus, Adelphi University

Chapter 17: Finding and Feeding Your Creativity 73
Dr. Drew Bogner, president emeritus, Molloy University

Chapter 18: Finding the Job of the Future 79
Dr. Drew Bogner, president emeritus, Molloy University

Chapter 19: Prepared for Work, Not Just a Job 83
Dr. Robert A. Scott, president emeritus, Adelphi University

Chapter 20: What Is Your Real Job? 87
Dr. Drew Bogner, president emeritus, Molloy University

Chapter 21: Voting Is an Act of Choice and an Exercise of Voice 91
Dr. Robert A. Scott, president emeritus, Adelphi University

Chapter 22: Thinking Globally, Acting Locally 95
Dr. Robert A. Scott, president emeritus, Adelphi University

Chapter 23: Acting as a Guest on the Planet 99
Dr. Drew Bogner, president emeritus, Molloy University

Chapter 24: Being a Pilgrim in Life, Not a Tourist 103
Dr. Drew Bogner, president emeritus, Molloy University

Chapter 25: Change Is the Only Constant 107
Dr. Robert A. Scott, president emeritus, Adelphi University

Chapter 26: Mentors Matter 111
Dr. Robert A. Scott, president emeritus, Adelphi University

Chapter 27: Being a Connoisseur of Knowledge 115
Dr. Drew Bogner, president emeritus, Molloy University

Chapter 28: Being Good, Not Great 119
Dr. Drew Bogner, president emeritus, Molloy University

Chapter 29: The Gift of a College Degree 123
Dr. Drew Bogner, president emeritus, Molloy University

Chapter 30: Navigating the Passage through College 129
Dr. Robert A. Scott, president emeritus, Adelphi University

About the Authors 133

Chapter Summaries

CHAPTER 1: LIVING A LIFE OF SUCCESS

The secret to success is living your life in a way that reflects who you are. There is no one definition of success and no one path to it. However, drawing from conversations with hundreds of successful individuals, there are six common attributes that were demonstrated in each of their journeys to a successful career and life.

CHAPTER 2: GETTING THE MOST OUT OF COLLEGE

Getting the most out of college requires that we match our interests, motivation, and abilities to an institution's culture, its commitment to student services, and its approach to student development. We consider "approach" in most other endeavors, whether in sports, clubs, or romance. Likewise, we should consider the approach of those who would educate us or our family. Indeed, we should understand our own approach to education. In this chapter, we will explore an approach to college success.

CHAPTER 3: FINDING AND USING YOUR VOICE

What is the key to being successful in college? It is being engaged in class and our deciding to be active and involved in purposeful learning. In this way, students can overcome shyness. They can become more poised in groups, develop a passion for ideas, and pursue concepts and subjects that lead to a successful career. While before college, experiences for individual expression can be few and far between, one of the important goals of advanced education is to develop students' critical thinking and communication skills.

CHAPTER 4: DON'T LISTEN

How do we go about identifying our dreams and work to achieve them? As surprising as it may sound, the key, Martin Short's character, Jiminy Glick, once told the authors, is "not listening." Don't listen to those voices coming from others; listen to your own internal voice.

CHAPTER 5: WHAT ARE THE LIBERAL ARTS, ANYWAY?

The liberal arts and sciences are about questions and imagination, historical context, and interpersonal relationships. Liberal education is not about a political leaning. Its root meaning is freedom, the freedom to question and learn. Its goal is to teach the ordinary student to become a cultured person and to appreciate other cultures, to develop the capacity to assess assumptions and understand the value-laden choices that await them as citizens, consumers, and arbiters of ethical alternatives.

CHAPTER 6: SYLLABUS FOR YOUR LIFE

We make hundreds of decisions in a week, many without seeking information from reputable sources. What would happen if we were more intentional about acquiring knowledge as a means to being more intentional about shaping our own lives and the world?

CHAPTER 7: HOW DO WE KNOW WHAT WE THINK WE KNOW?

We live in a world of competing truths and facts. How do we know what we think we know? People come to a truth through fact, faith, or fear. Each of these ways of coming to a definition of truth must be acknowledged as being real and important to the individual. Our survival as a democracy requires that we work together and stop disparaging others with whom we disagree. We must find ways to move people to an understanding of truth based on facts while acknowledging their beliefs and fears. In this chapter, we describe one process for disagreeing without being disagreeable.

CHAPTER 8: LET YOUR LIFE SPEAK

What does it mean to live a meaningful life? The finite reality of time teaches us to ask two important questions: Is what I am doing right now how I want to spend my time? And what do I want my legacy to be? The legacy you will build is built one day at a time. The decisions we make every day about how to treat others, how to spend our time, and what we choose to do become our legacy.

CHAPTER 9: HOW SHOULD I SERVE OTHERS?

Can we allow ourselves to be silent in the face of social and economic injustice, or unethical behavior and discrimination? As citizens, we must employ the ethical eye to observe and challenge societal patterns that test our sense of what is just, and be a person who displays common courtesy, respect, civility, and compassion.

CHAPTER 10: WHO DO YOU WANT TO BE?

What are the universal values necessary to define who we want to be? Is it respecting the dignity of each individual, being ethical in our behaviors, and being seekers of truth and justice through evidence, not emotion? We are called to be educated citizens who make a commitment to be lifelong, self-reflective learners.

CHAPTER 11: TRUST YOURSELF

When preparing for decisions, we have choices to make, and some choices have more serious consequences than others. But if we trust ourselves, if we have reasonable self-confidence in the probabilities of the correctness of our decisions, if we have considered the alternatives and have confidence in our choice, we can move forward. Trust yourself.

CHAPTER 12: CHOICES AND DECISIONS

There are so many decisions that we make each day. Of these, what are the most important decisions that one needs to make in life, and how do we keep these choices and decisions in the front of our mind? What will be your legacy and how will you leave the world better than you found it?

CHAPTER 13: WHY DIVERSITY MATTERS

We live in a world of increasing diversity. Why does diversity matter, and why should we embrace it in the workplace? Aside from the philosophical basis that respecting diversity is the fair and ethical thing to do, there are pragmatic reasons for fostering diversity. Embracing diversity in the workplace allows companies to be more competitive. Experiencing diversity in a person's individual life allows a person to expand their horizons and see and understand what makes the world a complex but interconnected whole.

CHAPTER 14: WHAT YOU SAY MATTERS

Words are indeed powerful. What you say, how you say it, and when you say it can have positive or negative consequences. Since you decide what to say and when, you have the power to influence situations and others' behavior. How will you use this power?

CHAPTER 15: BEING AN EFFECTIVE LEADER

Many scholars and successful leaders agree on the characteristics that are essential for being an effective leader. Leaders challenge the process, inspire a shared vision, enable others to act, model the way, and encourage the heart. How can we apply these lessons to leadership opportunities in our own lives?

CHAPTER 16: DEVELOPING LEADERSHIP SKILLS

One of the secrets to being an effective leader is listening with the eyes as well as the ears. Good leadership relies on being self-aware, understanding the different ways that people come to know the truth of a situation and form assumptions. Making change happen relies on knowing how to understand and validate others' assertions and assumptions as the starting point for shaping and altering them.

CHAPTER 17: FINDING AND FEEDING YOUR CREATIVITY

The need to create is deep within each person. How do we attend to this need to be creative and make time for this fundamental human characteristic within our hectic daily lives?

CHAPTER 18: FINDING THE JOB OF THE FUTURE

How do we prepare for a world that does not exist yet? How do you prepare for a job or a career in this unfolding world? In addition to specific skill sets for specific jobs, we must acquire and demonstrate certain character traits and abilities such as personal interaction skills, communication skills, and information and digital literacy. All these skills and abilities are essential for both current and future jobs and careers.

CHAPTER 19: PREPARED FOR WORK, NOT JUST A JOB

Jobs disappear, disrupted by technology or policies. But work expands; it is ever present. We must prepare students for a future in which they see themselves as problem solvers in constantly evolving settings for work.

CHAPTER 20: WHAT IS YOUR REAL JOB?

You will be asked many times the question, "What do you do?" Usually, most people will answer the question by telling the person what job they hold. However, in life, the answer to the question is about much more than an occupation. It is about what you do for others, for society, and to impact our world. Citing a conversation with congressman and civil rights activist John Lewis, the question is posed, "For what cause will you be an activist?"

CHAPTER 21: VOTING IS AN ACT OF CHOICE AND AN EXERCISE OF VOICE

Voting is a fundamental element of democracy. It gives us a chance to choose between candidates and is an opportunity for us to express our opinion and our voice. Unfortunately, many people do not fulfill this responsibility and others act to restrict who can vote. We need to act so that the act of choosing remains possible.

CHAPTER 22: THINKING GLOBALLY, ACTING LOCALLY

Increasingly, we live in an interdependent world. Through electronic telecommunications and jet travel, ideas, currency, and disease can travel in uninterrupted ways. It is important to know that most of what is local is affected by global forces and that global outcomes can result from local actions.

CHAPTER 23: ACTING AS A GUEST ON THE PLANET

How might the planet and its diverse ecosystems survive and thrive if we acted more like a guest rather than an owner of the earth?

CHAPTER 24: BEING A PILGRIM IN LIFE, NOT A TOURIST

We can choose to be a tourist in life, moving from one task or event to the next, or as a pilgrim who is open to the journey of life. The pilgrim concentrates on the immediate moment, having gratitude for all one sees and meets, letting go, and letting God happen. The choice of how you approach life is up to you.

CHAPTER 25: CHANGE IS THE ONLY CONSTANT

Managing change requires knowledge, understanding, and continued improvements in skills, abilities, and values. Many leading thinkers and opinion leaders have been sideswiped by change. What in the world could Ken Olsen, a pioneer in computing, have meant in 1977 when he said, "There is no reason for any individual to have a computer at home"? And what did Thomas Edison have in mind when in 1922 he said, "The radio craze . . . will die out in time"? As they say, "Nothing is permanent except change. . . ."

CHAPTER 26: MENTORS MATTER

We do not succeed on our own. There are always others, mentors who guide, shape, and influence how we approach life and what we become. Who are the mentors you have had in your life? Why did they matter to you? Where are the opportunities for you to be a mentor to others?

CHAPTER 27: BEING A CONNOISSEUR OF KNOWLEDGE

What does it mean to be educated? Does it mean that you know a lot about a little or a little about a lot? Perhaps it is both, but more so, it is about becoming a connoisseur of knowledge, knowing which concepts or theories to pair with specific situations to heighten awareness.

CHAPTER 28: BEING GOOD, NOT GREAT

Joseph McNeil was a college freshman when he walked a few blocks from his college to a Woolworth's store and sat down at the lunch counter reserved for whites only. This act of protest sparked a national movement that led to the desegregation of lunch counters across the U.S. As Mr. McNeil shared with the authors, he did not, through his actions, intend to be seen as special or great, but only to do, that day, what was right and good. We are all similarly called upon to be good and to do good.

CHAPTER 29: THE GIFT OF A COLLEGE DEGREE

Why did we build a system of higher education? What makes it distinctive? Why do we invest in it? Why do parents pay for part of it? Why do we spend taxpayer dollars on it? It is more than helping individuals to become employed. It is educating a knowledgeable, active citizenry that will reimagine and build the future. College is a gift that a few generations ago was not open to most Americans. As such, each graduate has received a gift from previous generations that they are called upon to pay forward.

CHAPTER 30: NAVIGATING THE PASSAGE THROUGH COLLEGE

A passage is both a way of exit and of entrance. It denotes the passing from one place, stage, or condition to another. It is an apt metaphor for describing the path of first-generation students to college and the navigational tools they need to achieve success. While many of the ideas discussed in this chapter relate to students of traditional college age (eighteen to twenty-two), the advice applies to all. Take initiative and ask for help. It is when students remain silent, especially when facing difficult choices, that they can fall behind and let a slow start become a stalled start. Even skilled navigators need assistance to guide their passage to the desired destination.

Foreword

Carla Deazle, PhD

Who knew that the eve of my senior year would be both memorable and fulfilling for many years after? During the summer break of the year 2000, I was selected to take part in an interview panel to select the next university president. I was the former president of the NAACP chapter, president of my sorority, and an active student leader on campus. I never imagined that my leadership would present me the opportunity to serve on a panel tasked with selecting the ninth president of Adelphi University. Even more astonishing, just shy of a year later, I was on the brink of graduating from college when I was selected to speak at the inauguration of the university president. What an honor! What an experience! The man I interviewed and who would become my mentor was Dr. Robert Scott. What did he see in me then? What does he continue to see in me now more than twenty years later?

When asked to write this foreword, I felt the same immense honor as I did over twenty years ago. Now an experienced and accomplished professional, I must acknowledge the importance Dr. Scott contributed to my own student success and to shaping my career postgraduation. Dr. Drew Bogner and Dr. Robert Scott have written a book that gives students a candid yet thorough perspective on college success, the influence of educators and administrators as stewards in helping to motivate students to achieve their full potential, and the power that students themselves possess to affect their own successes.

When starting college, many wonder what it is to be a college student. *How will my college experience influence me postgraduation?* There is an inevitable reciprocity of learning and leading that is ever present in college. Having a successful leader as a model who can provide examples on how to lead—and give the reassurance and space to develop academic and professional success—is a plus. There is a continuous need for educators and administrators to meet students' educational interests and individual needs by making students feel heard and seen. They do this by implementing a curriculum that is diversified to attract and retain students and that can positively impact their sense of belonging on campus.

As a college student, you learn just as much outside the classroom as you do inside. Attending college in many ways is a "rite of passage" where you are asked how to think instead of what to think, and where learning feels like a partnership. Prior to college, there is a sort of academic restriction on how to think, how to write, how to sit, and even how to stand. Juxtaposed to this is college, where freedom to express what you think, synthesis and analysis of thoughts and personal perspectives, and learning how to substantiate personal perspectives is essential to finding your voice and taking the reins to ensure a successful college experience. Therefore, what does success as a college student look like? What can that success feel like, whether academically or through moving into leadership roles on campus? And how can the impact of strategically placed mentors help shape the successes of students?

The brilliance of this book is the honesty and digestible points made. Seeking truth and learning authenticity through thinking independently are integral for being a successful college student. Historically speaking, we know what the success and impact was for individuals such as Nelson Mandela, Maya Angelou, Abraham Lincoln, Ruth Bader Ginsberg, and other historical figures. Students should ask themselves what they want their impact and lasting impressions to be while in college and beyond. Students can effect real change through their knowledge and the wisdom garnered through their college and real-world experiences. Being educated gives students options and is a source of power toward self-actualization of talents and skills. Students should consider what they want their academic legacy to be. This book is timely and relevant as many colleges have a continued desire to improve attrition rates, increase student engagement, and ensure student success. Dr. Drew Bogner and Dr. Robert Scott present a realistic guide for students. They discuss both the historical and contemporary perspectives of college learning and how students can and should take ownership of their learning to gain a successful collegiate experience.

Dr. Carla Deazle was previously the director and assistant director of general studies, the first-year student program at Adelphi University.

Acknowledgments

Writing a book with a colleague and friend, like any joint endeavor, requires trust, clear communications, and mutual understanding of the goal. Fortunately, this has been our experience in writing *Letters to Students: What It Means to Be a College Graduate*. We have similar values and have enjoyed working together over the years, even when we were often competing for the same students, faculty, and staff.

In addition to thanking each other, we want to thank our agent, Nancy Rosenfeld of AAA Books Unlimited, who guided us in preparing our original drafts into a manuscript accepted by Rowman & Littlefield. The editorial staff at Rowman & Littlefield were helpful in preparing the final book. Along the way, we benefited from editorial assistance from Jan Civian, who provided a careful reading that helped improve the final product. We also thank Dr. Carla Deazle, an expert on college student transitions and success, who wrote the foreword.

We are grateful to our colleagues and friends who wrote blurbs promoting our book and gave advice on our approach. These include Dr. Jonathan Algar, president of James Madison University; Donald Boomgaarden, president of St. Joseph's University, New York; Bobby Gitenstein, president emeritus, the College of New Jersey; Edward Giuliano, president emeritus, New York Institute of Technology; George Martin, president emeritus, St. Edward's University; Edward Ray, president of Oregon State University; Stephen Joel Trachtenberg, president emeritus, George Washington University and University of Hartford; and Mary Lou Yam, president of Notre Dame of Maryland University.

The few chapters that were published previously as articles in newspapers and higher ed journals are reprinted with permission.

As longtime campus presidents who put student success as a top priority, and who remember the support and encouragement of teachers and professors in our development as people and professionals, we hope that those who read and use our book will carry on our commitment to student accomplishment and growth.

Dr. Drew Bogner
Dr. Robert A. Scott
December 2023

Preface

For sixteen years we served as presidents of competing institutions of higher education located within five miles of each other. While we attempted to attract similar students, we found that as educational leaders we shared a commitment to student success and the advancement of each student's potential. We both recognized, as well, the clarion call for our graduates to respond to the needs of the Long Island community and to make a difference in the lives of others. This book comes from the many conversations we have had, over time, with our students and graduates. Conversations about the purposes of higher education and the potential impact that our graduates could have in shaping the world and living purposeful lives.

As a college president, one of your primary roles is to articulate the role higher education plays in society and how it changes and transforms individuals, preparing them for a career and to be active, responsible members of a community. Over the last few years, we found more people questioning the value and worth of a college education. For some it had become a simple value proposition, weighing the cost of higher education and its associated debt against more immediate earnings from employment.

What this calculus fails to incorporate are all the other reasons a person goes to college. This book attempts to articulate the myriad of purposes for attending college and the varied parts of life it brings into focus for a person to consider.

Why do we go to college? Why do we invest four years or five years or six years or more of our lives pursuing a degree? Why do we or our parents invest so many dollars in paying for tuition or room and board?

Why do governments, both federal and state, on behalf of taxpayers invest significant dollars in supporting state institutions or funding scholarships and grants? Why do alumni and donors give nearly $53 billion each year to support colleges and universities?

The answers are both simple and complex. A college degree is still the single best investment you can make in yourself. It is the gateway to most professions and has become an important sorting mechanism for the hiring of many jobs.

Professions require graduate degrees or postbaccalaureate coursework to meet minimum qualifications, obtain licensure, or sit for certification exams. This is true for many professions ranging from pharmacy to physical therapy, CPA licensure, and gaining tenure in many states for teachers. These are just a few examples.

Many businesses use college degrees, both undergraduate or graduate, as a minimum requirement for job application. A bachelor's degree is almost a necessity for a middle-class life and steady employment. In our society it is seen as the place for the development of advanced skills and abilities.

Achieving career goals and obtaining employment are not the only reasons to attend college. For traditional-age students, enrollment is often seen as a necessary step in the transition to adulthood. It is a time when young people can explore and discover interests, hone skills, make lifelong friends, and come to understand how to relate to people of varying backgrounds and experiences. It is a time of growth and personal introspection.

It is a time for charting one's own path and becoming the person you want to be. The campus is a place to bond with others and form mentoring relationships. Personal growth is so profound during these years that many college graduates develop an emotional bond with their alma mater that is still strong years later.

For nontraditional students, college attendance may be more about career advancement than character development, but they too learn to become more fulfilled as individuals and more engaged in society.

American higher education is unique in placing almost equal importance on the personal development of the student as it does on instruction. We invest in extracurricular activities. We encourage students to live on campus and engage in campus activities, participate in clubs, athletic teams, service projects, and international travel; we encourage them to seek internships and take part in leadership opportunities. We encourage those who live off campus to be engaged as well. At American four-year universities and colleges, about 30 percent of the budget is devoted to instruction while nearly an equal amount is devoted to student life and academic support.

Reading college mission statements and strategic goals, one finds similar attention to these topics:

- Developing mastery of a subject, usually called a major course of study
- Supplementing the major course of study with a comprehensive general education program that introduces students to the variety of subjects in the arts, humanities, science, mathematical sciences, and social sciences
- Developing communication skills in both written and oral form

- Developing information literacy. that is, the skills necessary to find and evaluate information
- Developing analytical and leadership abilities
- Developing values such as teamwork, respect for others, and engagement in society
- Developing interpersonal skills that allow a person to relate to individuals from varying backgrounds and cultures

These all add up to an understanding of yourself—coming to know who you are and the path you want to follow in life.

The three functions of the university can be summarized as (1) "creator" of the new, whether new knowledge, understanding, scholarship, and other creative activity; (2) "curator" of what is known, being a repository of the past whether in books, discs, databases, plaster, or clay; and (3) "critic" of the status quo, asking, "Why?" and "Why not?," and encouraging critical thinking and independent thought.

Of these three, the creator function is fundamental and is supported by the other two. Student learning and talent development are at the center. Learning is advanced by a commitment to learning history and the historical method, that is, what came before, whether in politics or science; imagination, that is, having the freedom to challenge what is and consider alternative possibilities; compassion, that is, not only feeling sympathy for someone else's pain, or feeling empathetic for their suffering, but being moved to action in response to it; and reflection, that is, wondering what can be learned from an incident or lecture and asking questions. Through reflection, we come to understand ourselves, our values, passions, and talents. We learn to know who we are and the path we each want to follow in life.

These are the purposes and functions of a university education. Attending and graduating from college is about all these goals and more. The ability to attend college is a precious gift and a special time in a person's life. This is particularly true for traditional-age students who recently graduated from high school. As a society, we make it possible for many of these individuals to postpone full-time work, use dollars saved, take on debt, pledge future dollars, live away from home, and postpone the payment of rent. We also allow and encourage these students to take time to explore, perhaps to study internationally, and to socialize—to be collegiate. Why do we do this? What do we hope will happen to these individuals? What are we hoping to gain as a society from all of this?

Parents sacrifice by taking on debt, even a second mortgage on their house. Individuals take on debt, an IOU that will be paid in the future totaling $1.7 trillion to date for undergraduate and graduate education. As taxpayers we also support and pay for this education through our tax dollars and the policy of tax exemption. On average, higher education is the third-highest category of expenditures in a state's budget.

For what purpose are we making this investment as individuals and as society? What are we hoping to achieve for the individual and society? As college and university presidents for almost fifty years combined, we have lived with these questions, thinking about outcomes, extolling the virtues of education, doing what we can to ensure that it continues as a moral enterprise while working to increase opportunities for others to obtain a college degree.

For students and their parents, grandparents, and family members, it is a little easier to understand why they make these investments. They want to open doors and gain access to all the things in life that make it worth living. They want to explore and find a purpose, chart a course that is of interest and meaningful, and one that can make a difference in society. They want their student to live a life that matters.

They know that a college graduate is more likely than someone with only a high school diploma to enjoy better employment, income, and health outcomes and be more likely to vote and be engaged in the community.

There are, of course, benefits to society as well, and that is why we invest so heavily in higher education. Unlike the rest of the world, we have built a system designed to provide opportunities for access without regard to high school academic attainment, age, or the ability to pay.

The United States higher education system is extremely diverse, consisting of colleges and universities that are publicly funded, privately endowed, tuition dependent, and sponsored by for-profit companies. It contains some of the top research universities in the world, regional colleges, comprehensive universities, and community colleges, some being open access, meaning that anyone with a high school diploma or equivalent can attend. There are literally places for everyone, and there is no central Ministry of Education to mandate who can go where.

There is also a robust independent sector of private colleges and universities, ranging from some of the top universities in the world to small four-year colleges and a few two-year colleges. Access to these institutions range from highly selective to almost open access.

This approach to higher education mirrors the highly American ideals that it is up to the individual to make something out of themselves and that there are many pathways to achieve success. Therefore, higher education as a sector provides almost everyone the chance to attend and make it through college. Students can transfer in and out and try it again and again, not just in the immediate years after high school but many years thereafter.

In most other countries, students are tested in high school and tracked into vocational/technical postsecondary schools or, in much smaller numbers, into a university track. One can argue that the American model is different because it is based on the belief in our society that everyone should be given an opportunity to succeed and that going to college is an essential part of this process. Consequently, our higher education system has evolved into an enterprise of multiple purposes, with a variety of institutional types.

The investments we make as a society are supportive of the individual and their potential for personal development and societal contributions. It is about hope and promise. It is about building a workforce for the future, capable of identifying problems and designing solutions for today and tomorrow. It is also about educating individuals to be contributing citizens who want to build a stronger and more vibrant society. It is about inspiring individuals to care about and solve society's systemic issues.

It is about challenging individuals to accept the responsibility to be stewards of the earth and their own communities. It is about being well rounded, capable of appreciating the complexity of civilizations and their gifts to humanity. It is about being articulate, thoughtful, interactive members of society who know how to sift through the millions of gigabytes of information to find principles, truths, and guiding concepts. It is about working to better the world, starting with their own community.

Too often, it seems, the varying purposes of a college education are lost in the din of political discourse. In this book, through the letters written directly to students and college graduates, we remind them and ourselves of the wide-ranging personal development and transformation that can and does occur in college. Hopefully, we will also remind ourselves of the many reasons we, as individuals and society, support and invest in higher education.

—Dr. Drew Bogner and Dr. Robert A. Scott

Introduction to Students and Graduates

Dr. Drew Bogner and Dr. Robert A. Scott

This book is meant to be a personal journey of sorts—connected to the college education that you are experiencing, getting ready to experience or have experienced. Collectively we have worked on college campuses for over seventy-five years as administrators, faculty, and university presidents. Over this time, we have had literally tens of thousands of conversations and encounters with students and alumni. Not only do we believe in the transformative power of higher education, but we have seen it happen time and again.

College is a time to develop valuable skills and abilities for the workplace and your personal life. It is time to find and come to understand fundamental concepts that help us make sense of the varied phenomena of the world so that we might navigate it more effectively and wisely. We learn how to find truth amid the multitude of facts and opinions that are so readily available.

It is the time to try new things, to embrace new possibilities and attributes of ourselves and the world around us, as well as enhancing those parts of ourselves that we come to value even more deeply. It is the time to chart a path in life that includes occupation and career. It is also the time for building lifelong friends and relationships that are often based on mutual interests and worldviews. It is a time of self-reflection and learning.

Colleges and universities are organized to assist you in this journey. You are exposed to a multitude of different academic disciplines, of sets of knowledge, concepts, and theories that explain some aspect of life, of you and the world. For example, history, psychology, sociology, English, math, and science. These are sometimes called the liberal arts and sciences or may be referred to as the general education requirements. These reference back to the original history of higher education, when it was expected that an educated person knew about the full range of knowledge. Today it is less about facts and details, which are easily accessible, and more about the underlying theories, concepts, and explanations that each discipline brings to our understanding of and ability to navigate the world.

You are expected to select a major and attain a deeper understanding of a certain subset of knowledge, skills, and abilities. In many cases the major is connected to a profession or occupation. Those who choose a liberal arts major are encouraged to think about a career and occupation with colleges investing in internships, clinical placements, and career counseling to further this purpose.

College is also about learning the skills necessary to be successful in life in general, as well as in a workplace setting, so you are encouraged to develop communication and computational skills, to learn how to find and apply reliable information to all manner of topics, and to organize and effectively communicate ideas to others.

Colleges work to help you develop "people skills"—teamwork, leadership, appreciation of diversity, empathy, self-responsibility, time management, and an "other" centeredness. American colleges and universities are somewhat unique in their belief that the education and development of many of these attributes and skills takes place outside of the classroom. So much so that institutions have built a rich array of extracurricular activities.

What have we learned from our time in higher education and from all our interactions with those thousands of students and alumni? First, embrace the journey and make the most out of it. Try new things and be an active, thoughtful participant. Actually do the readings and let them inform discussions with others. Try new concepts and ways of thinking about life. Second, be open to possibility. Let your curiosity guide your time and say yes when opportunities present themselves. Third, be self-reflective. Allow yourself to spend time thinking about the larger questions that are presenting themselves to you.

There are many purposes to higher education, but ultimately it all comes down to you. The central purpose is the development of you, to help you acquire the knowledge, skills, and attributes necessary to be successful in life and career, to allow you to make a contribution to society and live a meaningful life. Granted, there is a lot packed into this aspiration, with some very important and profound questions that require self-reflection. How do you go about answering these types of questions? That is the purpose of this book.

What follows is a series of "letters" to you: potential students, current students, and graduates of colleges and universities. Letters about how to chart your life path, achieve your own definition of success, and live a life of meaning. Letters about how to embrace curiosity and a lifelong commitment to learning, getting the most out of college while you are enrolled and thereafter. Letters about how to make thoughtful decisions about important aspects of life. Letters about how to be a leader, find the job of the future, and be a mentor. Letters about how to attend to all those things that make us human, creativity, dreams and aspirations, as well as meaningful social interactions and relationships. Lastly, letters about how to live a meaningful life and make a difference.

These letters reference many of the various conversations we have had with tens of thousands of students during our years on college campuses. Letters, quite frankly, that we wish we had written then, but have written now to you, along with some questions to guide reflection. College is a unique and special time, for during these years, whenever it occurs in your life, you have made an intentional choice to focus on learning and everything that goes with it. So college students and graduates, in the open letters that follow, we hope to inform, challenge, remind, encourage, and attempt to assist you as you consider: (1) who do you want to be? (2) how do you define and achieve success? (3) what does it mean to be a citizen? (4) how can you help others? (5) what legacy will you leave to future generations? and (6) what does it means to be a college graduate?

Chapter 1

Living a Life of Success

Dr. Drew Bogner, president emeritus, Molloy University

What does it mean to be successful? Is there one common definition or do we each define it, to some degree, in our own way?

I have been around a lot of successful people. In many ways it is what we do as university presidents, ask these individuals to share the fruits of their success with our students and our institutions. From all of these interactions I have come to recognize that there are two commonly held conceptions or misconceptions about success. First, there is no one definition of success. Second, there is no one path to success but, nevertheless, successful people and effective leaders possess some common attributes.

The secret to success is living your life in a way that reflects who you are—that resonates from your soul. Attending and graduating from college is an important inflection point in life. It is a crossroads of sorts where we make decisions that lead us down one career path or another. Since your job encompasses half of your waking, conscious time, doesn't it make sense that your work and how you do it reflect who you are and your values?

We can, by the way we do things, demonstrate our values, our creativity, our drive, grit and optimism, our humor (if we have any), our respect for others, and our commitment to a purpose greater than ourselves. I believe that no matter what the job entails, we all have the choice to approach work in the way I describe, as a reflection of ourselves and our core beliefs.

Fundamentally, it is important to understand that the definition of success is a personal one. It's important to realize this, for your own personal happiness depends on this realization.

Society will try to tell you that there are some important indicators of success, for example:

- What job you hold
- Whether you get a promotion
- What college you attend or what college decal you have on your car
- The house you own or the car you drive

But are these really indicators of success?

When you sit down to think about it, what is most important in life? Is it whether you are happy, loved, do a job you like; whether you make a difference in the lives of others; or whether you can use your creativity and talent to make things better? It is important to spend time thinking about what your own definition of success entails and not buy into the trap of pursuing another's definition.

One exercise that is helpful is to do a life's résumé. It is similar to writing a résumé for a job in that you list certain things you've already spent time doing and things you've accomplished, but the categories are different—for these categories are the really important stuff and they're your own.

For example, categories like:

- Friendships and personal relationships
- Service to others
- Mentoring others
- Understanding and experiencing the world
- Developing expertise
- Creativity
- Leaving a legacy for the next generation

These are just a few possibilities. Remember, you control the definition of success that will guide what you do and provide inspiration for your life.

I came to this fundamental realization in my own life in my early twenties, when I was in medical school. One of the most important goals of my undergraduate college education was to get admitted to medical school. Being a doctor was a well-respected position, so clearly getting in was, in and of itself, a mark of success. However, the further I went in medical school, the more I could tell that it wasn't broad or diverse enough for me. I remember thinking that I was sitting on a shelf, for at least four years, so many parts of myself.

Between my first and second year I did a fellowship in the Department of History and Philosophy of Medicine, and it was here that my mind began to turn to the academic life. By that time, I had met my soon-to-be-wife Karen, and coming back from our honeymoon I told her that I didn't want to stay in medical school or be a doctor and she said, "Well, then leave." So, I did.

I don't look back on this time in medical school as a waste of time, for I completed the most important part of my life's résumé there. I met Karen. I realized even then as I ventured out on an unknown journey, that in addition to there being no common definition of success there was no one path to success. This is the second misconception about success, that there is one main pathway.

It seems that there are two philosophical approaches that dominate the discussion of how one achieves success. The first is the ladder concept. In this concept one sees success as a series of boxes that need to be checked or a series of rungs that need to be climbed. In this paradigm, to be successful in your career you need to move from coordinator to assistant director to director to senior director to assistant VP to VP and then to senior VP and CEO, and your salary, as an indicator of success, needs to go along with this.

In other parts of life, it might mean a starter home followed by a bigger house and then a second home, and so on. I don't mean to denigrate any of these actions but to rather question if the motivation is one of checking a box so that others can see you as successful.

The second paradigm for achieving success is that of a journey. This concept allows for individual variations that can lead to the same goal. Think of pathways: some are more direct and faster—and some are more scenic; sometimes you step out for a while to focus on something else that's important. In this concept you allow your heart as well as your head to navigate your progress.

Most successful people I know subscribe to this second concept. Getting to the top of any profession takes a lot of time, commitment, and dedication, so quite frankly you'd better love the journey and find satisfaction along the way. If you can't tell by now, I subscribe to this paradigm.

When I left medical school, I certainly didn't think, *I want to be a college president, so what do I need to do to get there?* After leaving, I didn't know what I wanted to do and I didn't have a plan, but I came across a book titled *Where Do I Go from Here with My Life?* by Richard Bolles. It was for career changers.

It involved doing two things: first, writing your biography of work and asking yourself some important questions about what you had already done in life, for example, what experiences in your past work life did you find most rewarding and why. The second task was to find out about various professions and job possibilities by going out and interviewing people in these jobs.

I did this and quickly found out how amazing and helpful people will be to those who are trying to figure out the best answers to important questions in life. I decided I wanted to make a difference in the lives of people and that I wanted to help others. I wanted to use my talents and abilities. I wanted to have mattered. I wanted to be valued for who I am and what I can bring to the world, and I wanted to help others to come to these same realizations.

So, I settled on education—isn't it the most noble of professions, for we help change society by empowering others to be agents of transformation? I had always loved history, and in addition to my undergraduate degree in biology, I had a degree in history, so I enrolled in a graduate program in history to become a professor of history.

I had this idea that if I was going to teach, I should learn about education, so I also dual enrolled in a graduate program in the School of Education in the Department of History, Philosophy, and Sociology of Education. In my second year of grad school, to make money, I took a job coordinating the biology labs at a community college. Soon I was teaching undergraduate biology using my forty-five graduate credits from medical school.

I finished my MSEd, dropped the history degree, and started my PhD in history, philosophy, and sociology of education. One Sunday morning I just happened to look at the help wanted section of the *Kansas City Star* and saw an ad for an assistant professor of biology at my alma mater, Kansas Newman College in Wichita, Kansas. I applied and was offered the job. After one year, I was asked to go over to the Education Department, direct the Secondary Education Program, and start a nontraditional track for those wishing to become certified teachers. The next year I became the head of the Teacher Education Program.

The following year a new president came to Newman, and I was asked to take over the position of dean of community education with the job of starting other nontraditional undergraduate programs. I did this job along with my old job as chair of the Department of Education for one year. Two years later I was asked to assume the role of acting VP for academic and student affairs, six months later becoming the VP for academic affairs. I came to Molloy College as president nine years later.

One of the great things about being a college president is that you can talk to many different people, including many who have achieved what most others would consider to be success. For several years, I hosted a series of luncheons for successful alumni to spend time with our students who were pursuing a similar major. From all those conversations I concluded that most successful people did not follow a linear path to success. Many were like me. They tried multiple avenues or had jobs in a variety of fields before they settled on a career or a primary focus of life. I share this with you because it illustrates some of the fundamental attributes that I have learned from my own life and that of others that contribute to success.

First, every successful person I know is open to new opportunities and challenges. Invariably each was asked at some time, as I was, to take on new responsibilities or a new project. Usually, it meant a greater time commitment; sometimes it meant more stress without in many cases more compensation or a guaranteed promotion. The motivation for most was the same: the request meant an opportunity to learn, to grow, to use new skills, and to develop as a person.

Next, all these people say yes, and in many ways, this is the secret to success—saying yes to the myriad of opportunities that come our way. When we are asked to volunteer for a project or take on other responsibilities, do we see it as a burden or an opportunity? I think back on my journey and to every request that was ever made of me, and I always said yes. I didn't think about the compensation or the extra time. I thought instead about what good my new responsibility could bring to the college, the students, or the community.

Third, every successful person I know has a high tolerance for risk. Each is ready to hold the possibility of failure in their hands as they work to get something done.

Next, every successful person I know has grit. Grit is a characteristic that marries two fundamental mindsets: a belief in yourself and your abilities and a commitment to see something through to the end.

I can still hear my dad telling me, "When you say you will do something, you make a commitment to others and yourself that you will see it through to the end." Research indicates that grit is one of the most essential personal characteristics that allow individuals to rise above their circumstances.

Fifth, most every successful person I know realizes that you can't do it alone. Each can identify one or more mentors who believed in them and encouraged them to take on new challenges. These individuals also surround themselves with others who have a can-do attitude. Lastly, when they "made it," they reciprocated by mentoring others.

To recap from my own personal experience and from my conversations with hundreds of successful people, the pathway to success means:

- Being open to opportunities and new challenges
- Saying yes to these opportunities when they come your way
- Being willing to risk
- Cultivating grit
- Realizing that you do not do it alone—find mentors and good companions to accompany you on your journey
- Joining others on their journeys as a mentor or companion

Being successful and living a life that speaks to your soul is an intentional act or, rather, a series of intentional acts that involve reflective insight. It requires an understanding of your core beliefs, and this requires reflection and conversations of significance with those you trust, mentors, soulmates, confidants, and good friends. It requires being purposeful, but also being open and willing to take risks. Most of all, it requires listening to that voice inside yourself and not all the voices that you hear in society that try desperately to bend the arc of your life.

As my life has progressed, I have come to understand that the search for self is the most important quest one undertakes: coming to know your core beliefs that form the bedrock for future decisions, what makes you happy and fulfilled, how you want to spend your time, who you want to claim as friends, and the legacy you will leave to those who follow. These are important questions that deserve a place and time for reflection. Remember you define your own success, no one else.

QUESTIONS FOR REFLECTION

1. What are the important categories that you want to include in your life's résumé now and in the future?
2. Of the many opportunities that are currently available to you, which ones are worthy of a yes?
3. Where in your life do you need more grit?

Chapter 2

Getting the Most out of College

Dr. Robert A. Scott, president emeritus, Adelphi University

For many students, being at college, even part-time, is the first time they experience real freedom. Living at home or not, they are less likely to have someone to remind them of homework. If they live on campus or in an off-campus apartment, students have the freedom to associate with whomever they wish, skip meals, and otherwise experiment with their new independence. They can sleep late, skip class, and play pool instead of studying physics. Many have no one to urge them to pick up their clothes (other than a fussy roommate), no one to say, "Eat your breakfast" or "Stand tall," and other admonitions such as "Be home by midnight."

However, with freedom comes responsibility. Students are responsible for keeping up with assignments and requirements, class attendance, and part-time jobs. They learn they should not take five history courses at once, given the requirements for reading and writing and the need to fulfill other requirements. They need to know how to maintain their grants and scholarships if they are lucky enough to have them. Students also owe it to parents and family members to stay in touch, perhaps offering a brief report on knowledge gained and lessons learned.

One responsibility is to take full advantage of the opportunities offered by college, even if the student lives at home. Colleges are generally more diverse in demographic characteristics than the high schools from which students graduated. They can meet people from new parts of their state and country and from other parts of the world. Colleges also sponsor internships, study abroad, and other experiences in different cultures. Most campuses provide opportunities for volunteering in low-income neighborhoods and multicultural regions so that students can experience how to "do good" while also developing skills and abilities. It is incumbent upon students to take advantage of their environment and expand their horizons.

An often-overlooked opportunity is getting to know faculty and staff as individuals, not just as authority figures. Most became educators because they care about learning and nurturing younger learners. Many had an influential mentor in their lives. The stories of their professional journeys can be instructive as well as inspiring. Ask them how they got "to here from there."

The college years also are a time to develop the habits of citizenship: being informed; being involved in a community; learning to disagree without being disagreeable; promoting the common good; assessing the accuracy of information; rejecting violence; valuing the norms of democracy, such as voting and the transfer of power between administrations; and knowing what patriotism means. These, too, are important lessons, whether learned in or out of class.

Much attention is given to learning specialized knowledge in a major course of study and being introduced to a broader survey of subjects through general education requirements. College is a time to develop the skills of writing and speaking as well as the abilities of reasoning and leadership. It is in college that we can foster the development of values such as teamwork, fair play, and respect for others.

One of the most important lessons to learn in college is to reflect: reflect on a course, or an incident, or a ceremony, or a lecture. Students learn to ask, "What did this mean?" "What did I learn from this?" "Why is this important?" "How does this relate to or reflect on a historic issue or incident in politics or literature?"

College students learn about themselves through personal reflection as well as through instruction. This includes finding the optimal environment for challenge and comfort. We want college to be challenging so that we can improve in our skills and abilities but also want it to be a safe environment in which people care about one another.

Many students learn nonacademic skills that can last a lifetime, such as tennis or chess. They also develop lifelong habits of reading the news and reading for fun. They learn the value of time management and that it makes sense to ask for help. They master the value of work by seeking a job on campus where they are more likely to be supervised by people who care about their education and progress as students.

Equally important, they should master their finances, learn how to balance a bank account, and understand the implications of debt. The financial aid office staff can be helpful even if you do not have institutional grants and loans. They know higher education finance and want students to be secure. They want them to succeed and graduate.

Many students become involved in student government and get to know the student affairs staff. Those who live on campus can get to know the residence life staff. These are important guides to the college experience, what to avoid and what to emphasize. In my experience, these staff are most helpful in discussing the management of relationships, an important lifelong responsibility.

College also is a safe space to learn the value of taking an action. This may take the form of protest about a college policy, visiting the president to voice objection to an action or lack of action by the board of trustees, or writing letters to newspapers and local officials advocating a carefully considered position on public policy.

Issues such as the Sustainable Development Goals of the United Nations, climate change, racial justice, and access to affordable housing, good nutrition, and adequate schools locally as well as globally motivate students to be informed and involved. Students also join or create political campaigns for candidates and policy positions. This is a time of personal growth and becoming an independent person.

The college experience is a precious one, whether one lives at home and commutes or lives on campus. It helps us develop as individuals who learn how to manage freedom with responsibility.

Getting the most out of college requires that, in our college search, we match our interests, motivation, and abilities to an institution's culture, its commitment to student success, its approach to student development. We consider "approach" in most other endeavors, whether in sports, clubs, or romance. Likewise, I believe we should consider the approach of those who would educate us or our family. Indeed, we should understand our educational goals and learning styles.

I express my approach, my philosophy of education, by using several words that begin with the letter *I*. The key words are simple; they are inquiry, integration, involvement, independence.

By *inquiry*, I mean the spirit of inquisitiveness. This means that students and teachers should ask those fundamental questions asked by journalists everywhere: who, what, where, when, why, and how? These are questions to ask at the end of each chapter, at the end of each class session, at the end of a conversation. We should be inquisitive to deepen our understanding as well as our knowledge. Closely related to the spirit of inquiry is the application of imagination. We can improve the questions we ask by imagining that we are in the other person's shoes, and by imagining the subject from another viewpoint. By inquiring and imagining, we show that we approach every subject with serious intent.

The second key word starting with *I* is that of *integration*. Too often teachers, and consequently students, think of knowledge as belonging to a special compartment: English in the English box, and math in its own section. This, of course, is not the way professionals think. As professionals, we draw upon our knowledge and experience in a variety of fields. We address a topic in economics by considering historical and behavioral questions with the perspective of history and psychology. This is what we mean by integration—we help students see the interconnectedness, the interdisciplinarity of subjects. We emphasize this through our teaching methods, the design of our courses, even the makeup of our programs.

The third word beginning with the letter *I* is *involvement*. John Dewey was correct: we learn by doing. We learn by exercising our talents, by using both our knowledge and our analytical skills, by expressing our ideas, by assuming positions of leadership, and by participating. To be involved is to be fully engaged, emotionally as well as intellectually.

Too often students at colleges and adults in communities stay at home and do not contribute to the greater good. They not only deny their talents to the community, but also they fail to hone their skills and build their reservoir of experience. We know that students learn best and succeed more when they are involved. We should encourage involvement and exploration. As Swedish designer Josef Frank said, "The world is a book and they who stay at home read only one page."

Furthermore, through engagement and exploration, we will learn more about ourselves as persons. T. S. Eliot captured this notion when he wrote, "We shall not cease from exploration, and the end of our exploring will be to arrive where we started and know the place for the first time."

The sum of these steps is the fourth *I*, independence as an individual. Inquisitiveness, integration, and involvement all contribute to our becoming an independent person, one who in many ways is more fully human, aware of our desires and our biases. Independent, though, does not mean distant or aloof from others. An independent person is one who has confidence in their abilities, is willing to ask for help and to give it, and is committed to the broader community as well as to personal interests.

We become more complete as individuals because of the experience in a family group or other nurturing arrangement. We become more fully independent individuals when we are inquisitive, when we exercise our imagination, when we do not allow our thoughts, experiences, and observations to be limited to separate compartments. We become more fully complete when we contribute to the betterment of society, whether it be in our dormitory, campus, neighborhood, community, state, or nation.

These four key words are the building blocks for an effective undergraduate education. They help prepare graduates in character and for citizenship as well as for careers and commerce. Students who apply all four will benefit fully and get the most from their college education.

QUESTIONS FOR REFLECTION

1. How will you endeavor to be more inquisitive?
2. What about college do you think will be most important in five to ten years?
3. How would you describe your college experience to a sibling, cousin, or neighbor?

Chapter 3

Finding and Using Your Voice

Dr. Robert A. Scott, president emeritus, Adelphi University

Many higher education leaders say they are "student centered," and I am no exception. In my case, my commitment to student success was recognized by the naming of the Student Center at Ramapo College and a scholarship fund at Adelphi. The origin of my commitment is easy to discern. It was the teachers and professors who guided me, and I have been passing on their approach.

In eleventh grade, while other students were contemplating college plans, I was uncertain of my future. Neither of my parents had gone to college. My mother had died when I was nine and my father had suffered a bankruptcy. He was a single parent with two young children.

One day, my tenth-grade biology teacher, in whose class I had earned a rare A, had stopped me in the hallway and asked, "Bobby, why haven't you signed up for the SATs?" Why, indeed? No one had encouraged me. The guidance office, knowing my family circumstances, had urged me to apply to an inexpensive, unselective midwestern public university that didn't require scores and was hungry for out-of-state students. I took the SATs, earned a scholarship to Bucknell University, and the rest as they say, is history—a history whose critical "hinge" was a teacher whose class I had taken a year earlier and who cared enough to encourage me.

College was a starting point for me in many ways. My "well" of experience was enriched by the people, ideas, interactions, responsibilities, opportunities, and challenges it provided. It was in college that I became dedicated to a life of learning, the importance of questions, and writing as well as speech for communicating ideas. It was there that some lasting ideas about liberal arts education were formulated and guided later decisions as a dean and a president.

However, I almost didn't go and then I almost didn't stay. As a sophomore, I had doubts about why I was in school and whether I could afford it. Fortunately, my English professor and advisor talked me into rethinking my decision to leave and urged me to see the dean about additional scholarship assistance. Together, they helped me determine how I could stay financially and why I should stay intellectually. I have been indebted to them ever since.

I entered college intending to become a minister and graduated four years later with a job in management training at Procter & Gamble (P&G). After a year and a half, I entered the U.S. Naval Reserve as a trainee in cryptography and then became a trainer in the cryptography school. Because I enjoyed teaching and found it an invigorating respite from my daily routine, I paid dollars for others to take my duty watch so that I could teach English at the University of the Philippines center at my base—where I was paid in pesos, or twenty-five cents on the dollar.

During my navy service, I met many younger men (no women) in the barracks, dining hall, and computer-supported communications center. These young people had enjoyed little academic success in high school, even though they were curious and bright. They worked after school instead of playing sports or joining student organizations and were encouraged to join the military to "grow up." I quickly became aware that, for many of them, it did not take a four-year tour to become more mature and reflective. For many, it took less than two years. Yet here they were.

So, instead of returning to P&G or going to business or law school, I returned to my alma mater, Bucknell, as an assistant director of admissions, with plans to pursue a doctorate in sociology.

Several years later, fresh with my PhD, an associate deanship, and a faculty position at Cornell University, I began to imagine what I could achieve if I managed to become a college president. This was the position where people, ideas, and resources could be brought together to enhance the environment for teaching and learning. First, though, I wanted to learn about public policy at the state and federal levels, so I took the opportunity to become assistant commissioner of higher education in Indiana. There, I formed my ideas about higher education as an instrument for democracy—and the role of a campus president as chief mission officer, not just chief executive officer.

While in Indiana, I worked with leaders of small and large institutions, liberal arts colleges and major research campuses, single-site and multiple-campus universities, and both public and private colleges. I came to understand in new ways how higher education priorities and structures, as well as governing bodies, affected opportunities for student success. So, when I became president of Ramapo College, I called upon my sociological training to study the campus and the environmental influences on student satisfaction, retention, and graduation.

During my first month, I lived in a dorm room while my family was still in Indiana. Living among students provided a window into their lives and concerns as well as into facilities maintenance. I also asked the head of the theater department to study the campus as if it were a stage set. Then I asked him to give me a tour indicating where the promises in our mission statement were impeded or illuminated by our facilities and landscaping. I did something similar with the chief academic officer and deans in a review of the curriculum, graduation requirements, and staffing decisions. After all, I believed a mission statement is both a promise and a kind of script.

Later, at Adelphi, I enrolled in a freshman seminar in my first semester. One day during class I asked a student how she spent her day, where she "hung her hat." When she said that her car trunk served as her closet, I was surprised. So, after class, I asked the vice president for administration to tell me how many lockers we had for the fifty-four hundred commuter students enrolled at the time. When he said forty, I suggested that we tour the buildings and locate places for lockers and lounges. Not long after, we had hundreds of lockers and dozens of lounges located around campus.

At the beginning of each academic year, I helped students move into their residence hall. This gave me not only an opportunity to meet students but also to meet and talk with parents. Then, later that day, at the parents' reception, there were several dozen parents I had already met and with whom I could continue a conversation about how their students could gain the most benefit from the opportunities available.

On both campuses, I invited students, faculty, and staff to meet for breakfast, lunch, or dinner. I also met with them informally at sporting and cultural events. On each occasion, I asked two questions: "What is going well? What do you wished we had changed, added, or deleted last week?" I would then write up my notes and send them to the senior staff for discussion. Many important changes resulted, ranging from class scheduling, criteria for taking electives, food service hours, and mentoring faculty on the procedures for tenure, among others.

At each campus, the board's primary attention was on traditionally aged undergraduates. At Adelphi, I remember being criticized by a trustee because, he said, too few students attended basketball games. I became defensive, as the staff and I had worked hard to provide students with the complete collegiate experience no matter where their pillow was located, and many had theirs at home.

That evening, I returned to campus for a reception and a lecture by a famous author. The talk was well attended, with many students. As I left the auditorium, I saw a group of students in one of the meeting rooms. I peeked in and was invited to join a group of about eighteen young African American women and listened as they discussed relations with men and reviewed a PowerPoint presentation on male/female relationships over time. I was fascinated by the connection a student made between a 1940s newspaper advertisement that showed a white couple in a kitchen and a contemporary hip-hop verse. When I got up to leave, they invited me to meet with them again the next week.

After closing the door, I noticed in the next room a group of young African American men seated around a table. One of them saw me at the door and waved me in. I was enthralled as I listened to them discuss plans to tutor at a nearby junior high school and hold future sessions on how to be a "real man," and the fact that real men cry. They invited me to join them again.

When I turned to exit through the back door to reach my car, I was motioned by a staff member to come look at another room where about two dozen students were making origami pins with Japanese children to benefit a relief program. Again, I was fascinated by the degree of student engagement.

I had just seen about ninety students in total, any one of whom could have been at the basketball game. Yes, there was a game that night, but instead of attending it, these students were involved in initiatives designed to achieve a greater goal. I learned the next day that the young women were part of a newly formed group called FOCUS (Females of Culture United for Success) and were becoming increasingly active on campus. The young men were part of a group called MOCA (Men of Color Alliance) and they were active both on and off campus, working with younger students who faced many of the trials these more mature college students had conquered.

The third activity was related to a Japanese relief fundraising event to be held the next week, where students would be creating origami crane pins for purchase. The proceeds were to benefit the Japanese Red Cross Society by way of the American Red Cross.

These initiatives were inspiring. There were other student volunteers, of course, many organized through fraternities and sororities, and athletic teams, which set goals for helping others. What set that evening's activities apart was that they were spontaneous and individual, combining purposeful activity with group enjoyment. And none of these students attended the basketball game. They inspired me to think about the meaning of success.

Most people seem to think of success in terms of status, wealth, or power—in relation to others. I wonder, though, if this condition, "in relation to others," is necessary to understand success?

For me, success is the optimal balance of talent, time and treasure, and how we use and understand each in terms of status, power, and wealth.

By "talent," I mean how we use the gifts of mind, body, and spirit we have because of heritage, nourishment, practice, motivation, happenstance, and luck. No scholar, athlete, artist, or community leader of note is born successful. It takes circumstance and initiative to develop talents to their fullest.

By "time," I mean time for others as well as for self, time as the present and time as the future. A single-minded focus on honing skills, enhancing abilities, and accumulating knowledge may result in the maximum development of talent, but also may result in a life devoid of the pleasures that come from relaxation, reflection on our role in the world, prayer, conversation, companionship, and community involvement. Time is a scarce resource, just as talent is; neither should be squandered.

By "treasure," I mean that with which we start and that which we gain. Just as we can lose sight of important dimensions of life by focusing on achievement through talent alone, or by being selfish in the use of time, we can lose perspective—and sometimes integrity—by focusing solely on the accumulation of wealth.

Those who measure success through the size of bank accounts or the brand of cars and yachts, who keep score by counting currency, may know the price of everything but the value of nothing.

This is not to say that we should ignore financial rewards, or that money is somehow bad. No, it is to argue for balance in how we organize our lives.

In my view, the successful life is one that achieves symmetry in the attention given to the appreciation and use of talent, time, and treasure in the fulfillment of life's dreams and in service to others. Such a person knows that status, power, and money are measures used by others without regard to his or her own standards. As the Bard said, "to thine own self be true."

When I think about the mission of a college, I think of it as a form of covenant, a promise, and a marker on a path toward advancing knowledge, enhancing skills and abilities, and promoting values such as teamwork, respect for others, and service. This is what a college owes to its students, as I learned from my own teachers.

QUESTIONS FOR REFLECTION

1. What was your most important consideration in choosing your college?
2. Have you talked to relatives or family friends about their college experience?
3. What is your experience in expressing your ideas in writing or in a speech?
4. How will you use your time and talents?

Chapter 4

Don't Listen

Dr. Drew Bogner, president emeritus, Molloy University

One commitment we need to make to ourselves over and over again throughout our lives is to identify and work to achieve our dreams. Precisely how do we go about doing this? Let me begin with a story that highlights one important approach.

In 2011, at the grand opening of the new Madison Theatre on Molloy's campus, we held a black-tie gala event. There were six hundred people crammed into the lobby of the Public Square campus center dressed in tuxes and party dresses. The event was hosted by the comedian Martin Short. One of the characters he plays is Jiminy Glick, a rather odd and eccentric talk show host. In this role, Jiminy has interviewed a wide range of celebrities, and the plan was to get one on our stage for him to interview. However, for a variety of reasons this didn't happen and the day before the event, the office charged with organizing the gala asked me to be the "celebrity."

I said yes. I'd been interviewed many times before and thought, *How bad could it be?* That night, though, I looked on YouTube for videos of Jiminy Glick. It wasn't what I thought it would be like. His character was random and, of course, designed to make you look bad. He's a comedian, after all, and I was to be the straight man, the person to be made fun of.

I'm always prepared, and so I thought of a couple of questions I could use as a safety valve to ask him if I needed to buy some time. So, there I was sitting onstage when he asked me a question I didn't really want to answer. I don't remember the question, but I did fall back on one of my prepared foils. "So Jiminy," I said, "you're such a master of the art of the interview. What is the secret to a good interview?" "I just don't listen," he said and then proceeded to ramble on to another topic. Eventually, he came back to me and asked me a question. I paused and then said, "Sorry, what was that? I wasn't listening."

The crowd erupted with laughter and Martin Short broke character and gave me a high five. It was really just great fun, but after the show I began to reflect on the phrase "I don't listen," and realized that there was something really profound in that quip. The secret to success really lies in *not* listening. That's right, *not* listening. How, might you ask?

In a world where there is so much information, where there is so much thrown at you each day, much of what is important gets buried underneath the staggering volume of emails, text messages, tweets, and social media. If you want to be successful, you can't really take the time to read, review, or listen to even one-tenth of this stuff. Yet we are tempted to listen and respond to these "conversations." **Don't listen to these voices.**

There are also a lot of random opinions given out on so many subjects. These are everywhere. They will tell you that the economy is a wreck, that there are no jobs, and that the government is ineffective. They will tell you how really screwed up the world is. They will attempt to tell you what is realistic and what you should expect from your interaction with the world. **Don't listen to these voices.**

There are also a host of conversations where *you* are the subject. Observations about your future, about your abilities, about what realistic opportunities exist in your profession, about the type of choices you should be making now, about what is reasonable to assume and expect, given your stage in life. **Don't listen to these voices.**

There is one voice to which you should listen and that is your own voice, that voice wailing from inside you—speaking to you of your dreams.

"Dreams? Be realistic," some will say. "Aren't dreams just all blather and nonsense, unrealistic pie in the sky stuff?" But that is someone else talking inside of you. Your dreams are your dreams and, in that way, they are true and appropriate. The real question is how to make them become a reality.

To this, I say, seek out opinions on the how, not the what, and it is probably okay to listen to some of this. However, be an active listener; play it back through your own filter. Whatever you hear, you must ponder and weigh and decide, *Is it my voice or another's?*

Let me be clear, I'm not an idealist. I'm also not an optimist. I'm a meliorist. I believe that things can always be made better, that is, be ameliorated, but things just don't get better on their own. It usually takes focus and hard work. So, listen to yourself, focus on your dreams, and begin that journey in a purposeful way.

Jiminy Glick was right. The secret to a good interview, and to life, is not listening—not listening to the pundits, the naysayers, the pessimists, or to those who have little faith in the world or in you. Instead, listen to yourself.

QUESTIONS FOR REFLECTION

1. What is one dream that you want to commit to making a reality?
2. What are the essential steps to take to make this dream a reality?
3. There are many people who are willing to give advice. To which ones should you listen?

Chapter 5

What Are the Liberal Arts, Anyway?

Dr. Robert A. Scott, president emeritus, Adelphi University

Many of the most prestigious colleges are called "liberal arts" institutions. Universities often call themselves "liberal arts" institutions *at the core*. By this they mean that they require a general education of all students, no matter what the major subject of study. This means that students at nonselective regional colleges and those at the most selective national institutions can learn the fundamentals of history, literature, philosophy, science, and social sciences before embarking upon a specialty.

Many futurists agree that a liberal arts education is the best preparation for work, citizenship, and family life. They say that training is about answers—how to—and that liberal education is about questions and imagination. In ancient times, the liberal arts were known as the trivium and quadrivium, the seven useful arts, including rhetoric, logic, and quantitative reasoning.

So, what is a "liberal" education? Is it a political leaning? Or is it an approach to life's questions and professional challenges that continuously leads to new questions and understanding? I think of the liberal arts (and sciences) as liberating—freeing us from the provincial origins of time, place, and a single culture. The goal of liberal education is to teach the ordinary student to become a cultured person and to appreciate other cultures; to develop in students the capacity to assess assumptions and understand the value-laden choices that await them as citizens, consumers, decision-makers, and arbiters of ethical alternatives; to inspire students to contemplate the meaning of life and the role of religion, politics, and economics; to help students develop in their capacity to build a civilization compatible with the aspirations of human beings and the limitations of the natural environment; to apply theory to practical problems.

Liberal education helps students gain the confidence to formulate ideas, take initiative, and solve problems; develop skills in language, learning, and leadership; and increase their abilities for reasoning in different modes. It helps students to appreciate the pursuits of pure science and the difference between science and technology. It helps them fulfill their responsibilities as a citizen in a nation of immigrants. More than any other form, the liberal arts help us understand nature, the world we meet; culture, the world we make; and ethics, the systems of thought by which we mediate between the two.

With liberal learning as defined here, students can improve in clear and graceful expression in written, oral, and visual communication; organizational ability; tolerance and flexibility; creativity; sensitivity to the concerns of others; and aesthetic values. Liberal study in this way prepares students to weigh competing arguments and distinguish between and among fact, faith, and fear as ways of knowing; it frees them and us from ignorance and apathy. Liberal education fosters imagination, which Albert Einstein said is even more important than knowledge[1]—although I would add that knowledge of history, or context, is essential to imagination. Alfred North Whitehead said, "Imagination is not to be divorced from facts: It is a way of illuminating the facts."[2] A focus on imagination or "wonder" underscores the importance of the student and not just the canon. Liberal learning is the best preparation for what author Daniel Pink calls the "Conceptual Age"—the time beyond the information age. To succeed in this age, he says, we "will have to develop . . . our right-brain creative aptitudes to supplement . . . our left-brain logical skills."[3] Pink identifies six aptitudes needed: aesthetic design, story or narrative, symphony or synthesis, empathy, play, and meaning or purpose.[4] These aptitudes, I submit, are perfectly aligned with the liberal arts.

To fulfill its potential, a liberal education must also involve experience, in internships, voluntarism, and study abroad. Only then can the useful elements of the liberal arts be realized to their fullest before graduation, by using what is learned in one setting to define and solve problems in another.

This emphasis on liberal education should not suggest a lessening of importance on professional education. Indeed, many liberal arts colleges began by preparing teachers—by building professional preparation on a firm foundation of liberal study. That same philosophy continued in colleges and universities with the addition of engineering, nursing, social work, psychology, and business, and the expansion of graduate education.

The connections between liberal learning and professional preparation are revealed by the four key elements defining a profession: "an accepted body of knowledge, a system for certifying that individuals have mastered that body of knowledge before they are allowed to practice, commitment to the public good, and an enforceable code of ethics."[5] These elements are formed through liberal learning, as here defined, and the knowledge, skills, abilities, and values we gain from it. Liberal education is fostered in institutions that serve as curator of the past, creator of the new, and critic of the status quo. Liberal education is fostered in institutions that serve as curator of the past, creator of the new, and critic of the status quo.

Therefore, it is both liberating and conservative. It is about freedom but not of necessity about politics. It is the most useful foundation for continued growth as an individual.

QUESTIONS FOR REFLECTION

1. What is the origin of the term "liberal arts"?
2. In what ways does your college ensure that all students study some of the liberal arts subjects? If not, how can students pursue these studies on their own?
3. How are the sciences incorporated into the liberal arts?

NOTES

1. Friedman, Thomas L. *The World Is Flat: A Brief History of the Twenty-First Century.* New York: Farrar, Straus and Giroux, 2005, p. 441.
2. Bennis, Warren G., and James O'Toole. "How Business Schools Lost Their Way." *Harvard* Business Review, May 2005, p. 102.
3. Cornish, Edward. "Finding Success in the 'Conceptual Age.'" Review of *A Whole New Mind*, by Daniel H. Pink. *The* Futurist, September–October 2005, p. 47.
4. Cornish, "Finding Success."
5. Bennis and O'Toole, "How Business Schools Lost Their Way."

Chapter 6

Syllabus for Your Life

Dr. Drew Bogner, president emeritus, Molloy University

There is a tradition in the profession of nursing going all the way back over a century ago to Florence Nightingale, who placed a pin on those who had completed their nursing training. The pin symbolized that the graduate was knowledgeable and prepared to go out into the world and practice the profession of nursing. That tradition still exists at many collegiate nursing programs. In my tenure as provost and then later as president, I spoke at over fifty of these events, congratulating and challenging these new nursing graduates. Within my remarks I would remind these new nurses that one of the expectations of the profession, more of a requirement, was to commit to continually learn and stay up to date. For example, on medications, on protocols, on technology, on the structure and organization of health care, and on the theories and approaches of how to respond to the psychological and emotional needs of patients.

The same can be said of graduates in most any profession. Accountants need to stay current in tax laws and accounting protocols. Teachers need to stay current in the techniques and technology of teaching, in the understanding of the culture of education and the laws that surround, constrict, and shape or further the education of students. They also need to understand how to reach students of all matter of backgrounds, becoming a master teacher. The same can be said of social workers, psychologists, lawyers, managers, and most every profession, to learn the craft of it all, whatever it is, to develop and maintain mastery.

In our pursuit of mastery in our profession, we come to understand that there are reputable sources of knowledge that provide reliable and correct information and dependable and verifiable knowledge. There are consultants and workshops. There are articles in professional journals. There are books written by those who have solid and worthwhile experience, who help us to continue to learn and steer us to other information.

In many ways, after college, a person continues their education, relying on experts, somewhat akin to relying on faculty while in college. We don't seem to struggle with the concept of learning more about what is essential for our jobs, our employment, and our careers. In this pursuit of useful and relevant knowledge, we usually seek out the most reputable source of information, spending our time and energy to do so and learn.

However, we often do not apply this same approach to acquiring knowledge about so many of the other things that impact our lives. True, we spend about half of our waking hours dealing with work, but what of the other half? Sometimes, we do spend the time to do research before we make decisions. For example, before we select a movie or restaurant or purchase all manner of things from clothing to electronics to appliances to a place to live, we do our research, checking out respected sites, looking for what other consumers have to say, their ratings and comments. Sometimes we go to sites where individuals, whom some would consider experts, have spent real time investigating and testing the product. I know that when I search through one of our streaming services to select a movie or series and come across one that I don't know anything about, we check out the audience ratings and then go to a site like Rotten Tomatoes that summarize what the critics have to say.

We have also learned from experience the limitations of the experts, coming to know that in some genres like comedy, the audience rating is more reliable than the critics. We have also learned which family member and friend recommendations to rely upon, having been burned sometimes in the past.

Occasionally, I stop and think about how much time I have spent over the years researching movies and compare it to the time I have spent researching all the other things in my life. For example, the medicine and supplements I take, the people serving in office, the decisions that are being made by the local boards in my community, some of which will likely affect my neighborhood. Then there are all the decisions that could be made about how to build my retirement and where to make investments, or thinking what I eat and what it is doing to my body and long-term health, or what is happening in my schools, or to the planet where I live, or the judicial decisions that might affect me or the ones I love and who will come after me.

It is a long list, but it leads to one very fundamental question: What are the important innerworkings of the world that I should know about? What are those things that can or will impact my life and call out for me to understand and know them better? Lastly, what would happen to my life and the lives of others if I responded to them the way I respond to other parts of my life, spending time seeking out reputable and knowledgeable sources of information? For example, how would my life change it I did research on the things that I planned to eat before I went to the grocery store or ordered food at a restaurant? Similarly, what would happen to the world if I did research on the positions of candidates for office before I voted?! Each of us is given only one life. Do we want to approach it with some level of knowledgeable intent or let significant segments slide by with little consideration?

I acknowledge that it isn't really feasible to come to a working knowledge about everything in life, so, perhaps, it makes sense to start with a short list of those things that impact you the most or that will require you to make choices and decisions. For example, your health. Your health may seem fine now, at a younger age, but the effects of what you eat, the toxins that you expose to your body, and the lack or type of exercise you perform all add up as you age. So, consider deepening your understanding about what you eat and your diet, as well as how and how much you exercise, what to do to prevent disease and the effects of various toxins and harmful ingredients that exist in many of the products we use and consume. All of this requires some increased understanding of anatomy, physiology, health, and disease processes.

It also leads to the need to understand how the environment is impacted by various compounds and how all this affects us and other living things. This can lead to an understanding that the environment and other human beings can be impacted by the way in which things are made and what happens to industrial waste, and this might change how and what you buy.

If and when you have children or if you care about your younger siblings or nieces and nephews, you might want to spend some time following and coming to know what is happening to schools, including how they are funded, what is being taught or not taught, whether they are safe and how they could be made safer, and whether the schools will have what they need to tend to and take care of the students.

How do you make decisions about money? Do you have a budget? What do you know about investment and building a retirement and when you can and should retire? Have you thought about your student loans and how you will pay them off and or perhaps refinance them for a lower interest rate? What are the important things to save for? Will you set money aside for a down payment on a house?

These are just the beginning of a possible list. It could contain many other things, for we all live in a world that is complex, directly or indirectly impacting us and intersecting with our lives. We will be faced with many decisions to make, some thrust upon us, others consciously sought out and made. It is a surety that there are things happening right now that are impacting you or could impact you in the future of which you have little understanding. In an analogous way, there are decisions that you are making every day for which you have incorrect or limited knowledge and understanding. That is why I would like to suggest that we all engage in intentional knowledge acquisition (IKA). First, by making a list of what we want to learn more about and why and then allocating some time for doing this. This might mean a little less entertainment so that one can have a little more time for research and study, for learning. In an odd sort of way, it means continuing to do what you did in college.

The last step is to keep a log on paper or in your device of what you found. Log the key facts, insights, and suggestions of your research as well as a short plan of action. The findings of your time spent in IKA, intentional knowledge acquisition, will, I guarantee you, lead you into fascinating insights about other things and increase your curiosity as you come to live an inquisitive life.

Most of us know what happens when we are intentional about something. We shift our focus to it. We spend time on it and we often get better at it, whatever it is. The same can happen if we become intentional about knowledge and its impact on our life. If we turn our attention to even some of those things that are impacting or will impact the quality of our life and then make a commitment to learn and apply that knowledge in the decisions we make, we will see a return on that investment of time. In a related way, like an individual who has developed a commitment to ongoing exercise and fitness, if you do the same for learning and knowledge acquisition, you will develop a hunger for it. You will become curious about the world around you and in you and you will want to know more. Like that fitness buff, it will become a habit and, if you are intentional about it, the net result might just change your life.

QUESTIONS FOR REFLECTION

1. What would be on your list of the things you would like to know more about?
2. How will you make time for this research?

Chapter 7

How Do We Know What We Think We Know?

Dr. Robert A. Scott. president emeritus, Adelphi University

One goal of a college education is to foster critical thinking skills in our college years, careers, and community service. These are the skills, abilities, and attitudes necessary to ask questions about assertions and assumptions. Such skills and abilities are especially necessary when so many politicians and pundits seem to be anti-science, whether concerning the climate or COVID-19. Some even call the Holocaust a hoax. When thinking about these assertions and allegations of "fake news," one can wonder: How do we know what we think we know?

I often think of the biblical quote "The truth shall set you free," and its variants, including "The truth shall *make* you free." The latter is used as a motto at many universities as a secular declaration absent its biblical origins.

This is a fitting motto for universities because these institutions are chartered to pursue the ideal of truth in accord with facts. In fulfilling this mission, universities serve three distinct roles. They are creators of new knowledge grounded in objective study and independent research; they are curators of what is and has been thought, whether true or false, in books or databases; and they are "critics" pursuing questions that ask, "What if" and "Why not," and inquire about fair and just outcomes.

But how do we know what is true? I think there are three basic ways that people claim something as true. One way is through empirical evidence that is supported by findings of fact that can be replicated by others. This is the path by way of evidence. This way of knowing a truth is based on trial and error and controlled experiments. In this way, we can learn the biological origins, manifestations, and consequences of disease. Medical scientists and public health experts explain what they know from objective studies. Their findings can be tested by others and reported in peer-reviewed journals to minimize the potential for bias influencing results.

Another way to find truth is through epiphany or revelation. People know this kind of truth because they believe it, often because of religious inspiration and teachings. To say that someone believes something is true without empirical evidence is not to cast doubt on their conclusion or belief. Instead, it is to clarify the process by which they determine what they consider to be true. However, when such "received wisdom" becomes an orthodoxy that will not tolerate challenges, that will not accept questions or alternative views, it can limit communication, mutual respect, and understanding.

Still another expression of a truth is based on emotion, including fear and prejudice. These "truths" can be the foundation of hate and discrimination. When someone claims that Mexican immigrants are "murderers and rapists," they are expressing a prejudice, an emotional claim, a fear of the "other," not a fact supported by evidence. The claim is true only as an opinion grounded in bias, superstition, or fear.

Each of these ways of knowing—fact, faith, and fear—should be acknowledged. We also must understand that we cannot argue against an expression of truth held by belief or bias. These ways of knowing are not susceptible to reason, but they can be the subject of ethical analysis. Ethics is the process by which we analyze assertions. Are they unbiased, objective, and fair, or are they prejudiced, that is, prejudged?

We must expose the nature and character of assertions made or actions taken. As Supreme Court justice Louis Brandeis famously said, "sunlight is the best disinfectant," so we must expose falsehoods and fearmongering for what they are. Someone might assert that climate change is not occurring or is not caused by human behavior. However, such opinions should not stand in the way of taking steps to mitigate climate disasters when flooding and land loss are affecting fellow human beings.

Someone else might assert that wearing masks and social distancing are denials of individual liberty. But such an opinion does not give a person license to deny the rights of others who seek protection from a deadly virus by wearing masks and practicing social distancing and asking others to do the same.

One can argue with the scientists about how to behave during a pandemic and the extent to which human behavior is threatening our planet, but we must do so with facts, not opinions based on emotion or epiphany. We are not only individuals, but also members of a community.

By emphasizing the importance of facts, we may offend others who think they "know" a truth through another means. But they must honor our path to truth just as we must respect their right to an opinion or belief. Indeed, the very foundation of democracy requires civility, the willingness to listen to alternative views. However, we should not allow opinions to negate facts or prejudice to deny others' freedoms.

Why are our disagreements so disagreeable? Why does it seem so difficult to find common ground? Why can't we see that our similarities are greater than our differences? Don't we all start each day seeking good health, economic security, and continued growth as human beings for our family, neighbors, and community members?

And don't we agree that we have these opportunities because we live in a nation based on the rule of law and a constitutional order and a Declaration of Independence that not only guarantee certain rights but also contain the means by which we, the people, can create a more perfect union?

Because I believe in this nation and these principles, I am increasingly concerned by efforts to substitute political for expert judgments in public health, to ban celebrated and historic books because of the facts presented, and to deny historical truths like slavery and the Holocaust because they run counter to a preferred narrative. What can we do to create more robust but civil discussions about policies and history?

A youth development organization I know uses an approach that might show the way.[1] Founded in 1989 and based in New York City and Washington, DC, it serves students in some of the most under-resourced public schools. It teaches leadership and research skills through classroom-based learning, the arts, and community participation in order to prepare students to become college-ready and active citizens.

Because the group brings together youth from diverse backgrounds, it developed a set of guidelines to promote robust but civil discourse. These guidelines include "One Mic," "Safe Space," "Participation," and "Think Globally and Act Locally and Globally."

"One mic'" means that one person speaks at a time. They do not shout over each other. They value other voices. They listen respectfully to what is being said instead of waiting impatiently to rebut what another is saying. They critique the ideas and not the person.

"Safe space" means that ideas can be expressed without fear of retribution or vicious reaction. It is a space that is safe "for" exploring ideas, not safe "from" new thoughts. It does not mean a space where individuals are guaranteed protection from uncomfortable ideas. A safe space is one in which ideas can be explored, books discussed, and policies debated with freedom of thought and speech.

"Participation" means that everyone is expected to contribute to the exercise, the task, the program. It is the responsibility of each person to prepare carefully, participate actively, and be a partner in achieving a new level of accomplishment if not agreement.

Participation is the act by which the individual becomes part of a community.

"Think globally and act locally and globally" means that we can learn from others, even those in other countries, and that we should use this knowledge in our local activities. With the guidance of this principle, young people have learned what other countries do about topics such as health care policy, gun control, housing and nutrition, and race relations. Other topics include immigration, economic justice, policing, voting, and schooling. They then can discuss these issues with more knowledge and a larger context.

If these principles and guidelines can be employed successfully, and over time, by high school youth, why can't we adopt them for Congress, school boards, and other public and private settings? Let young people show the way to learning how to discuss and disagree without being disagreeable.

Our democracy, our society, requires truth and transparency and less divisiveness. We need our elected officials to reflect the will of an informed citizenry and to work together for the common good. We need to protect the principles of social justice and equitable treatment.

Our survival as a democratic society requires that we work together and stop using labels to disparage those with whom we disagree. There is no path to justice when fear and prejudice prevail, when some rely on alternative facts, and no one listens to contrary opinions.

Therefore, let us acknowledge that there are different paths to what one considers truth—some based on empirical evidence, some based on emotion or bias, and some based on belief. Furthermore, let us agree that each of us can hold our position without denigrating a way of knowing expressed by another, unless that belief or bias endangers others and curtails their legal rights. Let us be able to disagree without being disagreeable, using critical thinking skills in college, careers, and community service.

QUESTIONS FOR REFLECTION

1. How do you distinguish between a "truth" known through fear, a prejudice, and a fear known through epiphany, a revelation?
2. What is an example of a "safe space"?
3. Describe a global influence in your life.

NOTE

1. Global Kids Inc. www.globalkids.org.

Chapter 8

Let Your Life Speak

Dr. Drew Bogner, president emeritus, Molloy University

What does it mean to live a meaningful life? Not surprisingly the answer to that question varies depending on who you ask. In 2017 the Pew Charitable Trust conducted a study to find out how Americans answered this question. When asked in an open-ended question what made life meaningful, the most common answer given by seven in ten participants was family; next at 34 percent was careers.

The answers varied by education and socioeconomic level. College graduates were more likely to mention friends at 23 percent, learning at 16 percent, travel at 11 percent, and activities and hobbies at 31 percent. No doubt, the answer to the question might vary by age, but it is a question worth asking at any age, particularly once we come to understand that time is a limited but elastic commodity. For time can go by quickly or languish. We have all experienced this, but we also know that any and every event will end or transition into something else.

We age and so do those around us. We have careers, but eventually for most, these come to an end. This commodity of time has always, it seems to me, to be one that deserves attention, for it is finite. We will only have so much of it in our limited life. We all know this on some level, although we often live our lives as if there is a never-ending reservoir of time from which we can draw.

The finite reality of time teaches us to ask two important questions during our life. The first question is one we may or perhaps should ask ourselves unconsciously or consciously almost every day. It is the question that asks if what I am doing right now, today, or this week is how I want to spend my time. Granted, we often don't have a choice about how to spend our hours and minutes, but there are also many situations when we do. There are so many time traps, surfing the internet or social media, for example. We know the ways in which we can squander time and let it slip away. Could that time be used for another purpose, doing something that is meaningful?

The second question time presents is more long term in nature. It is the question of legacy. When I reach the end of my work career or the end of my life, what do I want my legacy to be? How do I want to be remembered? What do I want to have done with my life?

If you were able to fast-forward in time, travel to the future, and observe yourself at sixty-five, what would you want that person to be like? What would you want that person to have done with their life? What type of career, what jobs, what activities that impact society and other people? Did you do something that made a difference?

The legacy you build is built one day at a time over a lifetime. It is built by how we treat others, how we spend our time, and the purposeful way in which we define how we live our daily lives. It involves asking yourself some really important questions, such as: How do you define success? What are your most important values? Are you living out and accomplishing what is important to you?

If you want to really sharpen this conversation to today, one can ask, what do I want people to say after I leave a room or think about me after I finish a conversation, or when they read something I wrote or texted?

It is hard at twenty-five to know how to precisely answer the question of what you want to accomplish in life. For there are many jobs and careers that don't even exist today, and we may pursue opportunities that aren't even on our radar now. For example, I certainly had no idea that I would become a university president. However, we can solidify our value system, deciding on those behaviors and personal attributes that will serve as guardrails and guideposts to important future decisions. In this we can be intentional. We can choose to be kind, to be generous, to be helpful, to volunteer our time, to be dependable and reliable, to be polite, to be an activist for a cause, to only say good things about others and resist the temptation to tear others down.

All the decisions we make every day about how we treat others, how we spend our time, what we choose to do and say becomes our legacy. It is akin to the old Quaker saying, "Let your life speak." Let your life speak in the dreams you dream and the actions you take. The everyday part of your life will speak more loudly to others than traditional accomplishments, so let that part of your life speak clearly.

QUESTIONS FOR REFLECTION

1. For you, what does it mean to live a meaningful life?
2. How much of your time is spent doing what you consider to be important in your life?
3. What does success look like for you?
4. What are your core values? Are you living your life in a way that represents these values?

Chapter 9

How Should I Serve Others?

Dr. Robert A. Scott, president emeritus, Adelphi University

Over time, I asked my campus community to think about our roles and obligations as members of society and to consider what it means to be an ethical person in service to others. When we do this, we should ask: Can we allow ourselves to remain silent in the face of social and economic injustice? Can we stand by in the face of repeated manifestations of unethical behavior, discrimination, and misconduct in the public square?

We citizens must employ the "ethical eye" to observe and challenge societal patterns that test our sense of what is just. This takes courage, as well as compassion. Compassion is a key component in how we serve others. Many texts on leadership and service emphasize empathy, that is, feeling the pain of others. This is better than simple sympathy, feeling sorry for others, but does not lead to necessary action. Compassion is an act of service, not just a feeling about others.

Calls for "civility" are also key. They respond to acts of racism, bullying, and other forms of uncivil behavior. I think these cries for civility are calls for compassion and respect.

It certainly is true that racism, anti-Semitism, and other forms of prejudice are active in our society, denying respect to those who are the subject of discrimination and uncivil actions. Therefore, it makes sense for those who have been subjected to bias and incivility personally or historically to want respect. Indeed, I assume that everyone wants respect as a simple fact of his or her humanity.

We should assert in our schools and houses of worship, and especially in our homes, that others should be respected for their humanity even if they are different from us. But there is a difference between respect for humanity at large; respect for ethnic, national, religious, community, and racial groups in general; and respect for any individual in particular. Respect should be offered freely. An individual's actions should no more reflect poorly on an ethnic, national, racial, or religious group than a group's actions should reflect poorly on all of humanity.

Respect is lost by acting in a callous manner, by disregarding others, by insincerity, or by belittling the place and relevance of others. When a student or a faculty member or lay member of the public "demands" respect and does so in a manner which itself is disrespectful, he or she not only misses the point but also demeans the issue. However, individual respect can be regained through effort: by being sincere, expressing remorse, by acting as part of a group that is trying to be positive.

A school or college is a precious place. It is where truth in whatever form should be pursued without hindrance. It is where freedom of speech must be protected to the utmost. It is place where diversity—of background, ethnicity, nationality, religion—should be valued. It is also a place where civil discourse and respect for one another is essential if a full and honest exchange of views is to be assured.

Without common courtesy, ears are closed. When ears are closed, there can be no mutual respect. We must learn to disagree without being disagreeable. Those who shout the loudest for respect may gain attention, but then must work to earn respect.

The ethical eye helps us identify the principles required to find the truth that lies beyond the prejudice of racism by focusing on fairness, equity, and justice for all. No one should be an "other" to us if our education has succeeded. We are one species, with each member seeking to find a unity connecting head and heart, or compassion, and leading to respect.

I raise these issues of respect and compassion because of events that affect us all but affect some of us in more immediate and problematic ways. Think of Eric Garner, Tamir Rice, Walter Scott, Rekia Boyd, Michael Brown, and Freddie Gray, people we now know by name who were killed by representatives of the justice system. Each name represents one event among too many that can be recounted, Black youths, female as well as male, killed in cold blood. How should we respond?

Moral standards have been upended and upgraded because of the organized efforts of many Americans who argued that discrimination of any kind is unethical and unjust. The ethical eyes employed by these average citizens stared down an old law, an old legal interpretation, an old morality. Their acts forced others to consider fairness, equity and justice, compassion, and respect, in creating new laws and new standards of right and wrong.

This, too, is the benefit of education and an inspiration to serve others.

QUESTIONS FOR REFLECTION

1. How do you define respect?
2. What is the meaning of the "ethical eye" to you?
3. Have you ever witnessed examples of prejudice or discrimination? How did you feel? What did you do? What didn't you do?

Chapter 10

Who Do You Want to Be?

Dr. Robert A. Scott, president emeritus, Adelphi University

We live in an increasingly interdependent world and ever more diverse communities. You can see that in your own school. The richness of this diversity in which we have studied, played, and discussed the world, and the values new members bring, adds to our personal growth. They enhance our ability to understand and communicate with others as neighbor, employee, supervisor, and citizen. We learn to put ourselves in the other person's place, and try to imagine how they view the world, and us. We need to consider who the other person is—despite his or her ancestry, accent, age, or achievements—as we learn how to become who we want to be.

It is increasingly likely that the graduates of our schools and universities will either supervise or be supervised by someone of a different ethnic, national, or racial background. It is likely that the work of our employers and activities of our families will be influenced in profound ways by suppliers, customers, clients, and others who are of a different cultural background.

What, then, are the universal values necessary to define who we want to be?

Surely one value is that of the dignity of everyone. As the saying goes, "Dignity has no nationality." Cooperation is a universal value even when the drive for competition sometimes seems overwhelming. Recognizing the necessity of mutual interdependence is a universal goal. Other values that are basic to human beings would be the set of freedoms articulated by former United States president Franklin Delano Roosevelt. He summarized these universal values as freedom of speech, freedom of worship, freedom from want, and freedom from fear. These and related values are essential ingredients for an education designed to foster an ethical, peaceful, and conflict-free world.

While laws and norms of morality, that is, what is considered good and evil, may differ by culture, the discipline of ethics is universal. Ethics is the lens by which we examine legal codes and moral standards and how they are applied. This lens helps us analyze the treatment of others, seeking fairness as opposed to bias and justice as opposed to prejudice.

When we consider our roles as ethical persons, we must ask, can we allow ourselves to remain silent in the face of social and economic injustice? I think we must employ the ethical "eye" to observe and challenge societal patterns that in total and in summary test our sense of what is just. This takes courage as well as compassion, but it is our obligation as educated citizens to identify the fault lines in society and develop appropriate strategies to address injustices wherever they may occur.

The ethical lens helps us identify the truth that lies hidden by racism, xenophobia, or misogyny, by focusing on peace, fairness, equity, and justice for all, even those who fit, or do not fit, a certain profile. No one should be "the other" to us if our education has succeeded. We are one species, whether natives or refugees, with each member seeking a unity connecting head and heart, no matter their religious commitment, national membership, or political affiliation. We are one in the air we breathe and the land we till, and in our understanding of universal symbols such as the one for peace.

There have been numerous societal patterns supported by governments and institutions of morality that have been challenged: consider slavery and laws denying voting rights to Black and female citizens. Such laws have been amended or abandoned and moral standards upgraded because of the organized efforts of those who argued that such discrimination is unethical and unjust. The ethical "eyes" employed by average citizens stared down the old law, the old legal interpretations, the old morality, by forcing others to consider the dimensions of fairness, equity, and justice. The result was the creation of new laws and establishment of new standards of right and wrong.

As educated citizens, we must seek truth and justice through evidence, not emotion, even as we are passionate in the pursuit of both. In all cases, we must take the path to justice free from bias, emotion, and fear, even when it may run counter to family values, local customs, or political rhetoric.

The ideals of educated citizenship encompass the notion of a culture of peace and nonviolence and can be fostered at home and in school by linking the news, literature, history, languages, and songs to discussions of everyday and historical topics. This is enhanced by teaching critical thinking and writing, and by emphasizing compassion and cooperation in the face of multiple forces that give priority to competition.

Peace is not only the absence of violence but also the presence of conditions for human development. There can be no peace without economic development, no economic development without community development, and no community development without the opportunity for education. This is public policy as if people matter.

The mission of every school and university should be to advance students' knowledge, skills, abilities, and values necessary for understanding different cultures; for being tolerant with compassion; and for being a global citizen. Surely, this mission is consistent with that of the UN Charter: "To reaffirm faith in human rights, to establish justice and respect for international law, and to promote social progress and better standards of life, they have promised to practice tolerance and live together in peace with one another as good neighbors for the economic and social advancement of all people."

For these reasons, I value an education that helps liberate students from their limited view of humanity, including their own, without regard to age, station, or place. The building blocks for such an education are (1) history, that is, the study of what came before, whether in our country or in another, in politics or in physics, or elsewhere; (2) imagination, that is, having the freedom to challenge what is and consider alternative possibilities, including what it is like for another to walk in our shoes or for us to consider what it is like to walk in theirs; (3) compassion, that is, not only feeling sympathy for someone else's pain, or feeling empathetic for their suffering, but being moved to action in response to it; and (4) reflection, that is, the habit of asking, What does this mean? What can I learn from this? What kind of person do I want to become?

There are, of course, limits to what we can teach and require of students. Therefore, I emphasize that the mission of education is to enhance the ability of students to learn on their own as well as in groups. We can promise to prepare students to learn anything even if we cannot promise to teach them everything.

We educators must ensure that our students understand and appreciate that they are the "other" to many in this world. They must know that we need to know ourselves—the history, literature, and heroes of the rich diversity of peoples who contributed to the development of our civilization, our institutions, and our values—if we are to understand our commonalities and differences when compared to others. Without this knowledge of others and ourselves, we are left with ignorance, fertile ground for suspicion, fear, and prejudice. Only then will we really know who we want to be.

QUESTIONS FOR REFLECTION

1. Who do you want to be?
2. Who are your top three heroes?
3. What skills and abilities do you want to develop?

Chapter 11

Trust Yourself

Dr. Robert A. Scott, president emeritus, Adelphi University

When I asked a young college graduate about advice he would give to students and fellow alumni, he said, "Trust yourself." We then had a stimulating conversation about his high school and college paths, including advisors, mentors, and friends.

"Trust yourself" sounds like a simple admonition, but what does it take? It certainly takes self-confidence, that is, confidence in yourself based on experience in overcoming obstacles. Self-confidence derives from reflecting on past experiences and learning from critiques offered by family, teachers, coaches, and friends.

It is important to ask for advice, but this takes self-confidence. I don't mean arrogance or blind faith. Asking for help requires that we be willing to listen to others with positive attitudes. We can seek to be receptive.

Asking for advice does not mean "paralysis by analysis," that is, delaying a decision by seeking endless amounts of information. There is a saying that "the perfect is enemy of the good," meaning that seeking perfection can take so long and so much effort that we don't get anything done. We should instead accept a good outcome that can be a step toward a more perfect solution.

Many people think in terms of probabilities. What is the probability that we can achieve the outcome we seek? In this way, we can trust that we will prevail. This takes preparation and practice. In a way, we are always preparing for the future by reflecting on our experiences and building a store of knowledge about challenges, successes, and failures faced.

I had a mentor whose advice helped me gain confidence in myself. He was one of several, but he was especially helpful. He would say, when I asked about a decision I had to make, "Secure your footing before you extend your reach." In other words, be confident in your position before taking the next step. Take reasonable risks, whether deciding on an issue at work or on a new job. He would then say that this is good advice for life as well as for mountain climbing.

Mentors, teachers, and friends can all provide a network of supporters, those who encourage us in our efforts. They can help us retain or gain faith in our strengths, and our inner resilience.

I remember a time in junior high school when some wise guys called to me and said, "What are you looking at, kid?" I was always fascinated by people and was curious about these schoolmates who dressed in black and acted tough. I had seen them bully others and did not want to tangle with them. I also did not want to act scared. So, I waved to them and said, "Goodbye." I walked away and they were confused. I trusted myself that I could pull it off without getting into a fight.

As students, we have decisions to make. Should we join a fraternity or sorority? Should we join a club or a team? Should we study what we love or what our parents say will lead to a good-paying job? We can balance the pros and cons, weigh the alternatives, seek advice, but, ultimately, the decision is ours. We must trust that we have considered the alternatives and then trust in ourselves to make the right decision.

In our jobs, we have many decisions to make. Should we hire this person or another? Should we sign a contract with this vendor or that? Should we promote this person or not?

I trusted myself when it became obvious that I had to make some major decisions at Ramapo College of New Jersey. The governor had cut funding for higher education and agreed to union agreement to increase compensation without providing funding to pay for it. This happened in May, just weeks before the start of the new fiscal year. It was the equivalent of a 9 percent budget cut.

I did not want simply to cut all campus budgets across the board. I thought that was a path to mediocrity. So, I asked for advice about what to do and agreed with a suggestion to eliminate football. Attendance at games was minimal, and the coach was leaving for another institution. Without a coach and with the star quarterback on probation due to grades, the time seemed right to save a great deal of money and preserve academic integrity.

I figured the decision would be controversial, but knew I had the support of the vice presidents and the chair of the board of trustees. I also knew it was the right decision and trusted myself. A couple of trustees were unhappy, even though I had briefed the board three times, but the board chair supported my decision and prevailed.

I also remember a time when I didn't trust myself. I didn't intend to lose confidence, but the prevalence of opinion from others was such that I buckled and went against my instincts. As a result, I learned a valuable lesson: trust myself and my values. On another occasion, I asked approval from a higher up who took so long to answer that I lost an opportunity. At times it is better to ask forgiveness than permission.

For each decision, we have choices to make, and some choices have more serious consequences than others. But if we trust ourselves, if we have reasonable self-confidence in the probabilities of success of our decisions, if we have considered the alternatives and have confidence in our choice, we can move forward. Trust yourself.

QUESTIONS FOR REFLECTION

1. What there a time when you did not trust your judgment?
2. What is an example of a mentor's advice that you benefited from?
3. Do your friends ask you for advice? On what?

Chapter 12

Choices and Decisions

Dr. Drew Bogner, president emeritus, Molloy University

We live in a time of choices, in a time when there are so many possibilities, so many options of what to watch, what to read, what to see and do, how to spend our time and how to present ourselves to the world. Time is a precious commodity, and how we choose to spend it is important.

How conscious should we be about the choices we make and the time we spend and what it all means for the life we live and the impact we make on the world? Let's start with that most important, singular gift that each of us was given at birth: the gift of life. Each of us is unique, with certain genetic predispositions. These strengths are modified as we grow and adapt to and around life events, allowing each of us to become a unique force that has the power to change our own lives and the lives of others. We each have a way of approaching events with distinct personality traits that shape these interactions, but we still have hundreds of choices to make each day.

We make many decisions without giving them much thought, for example, what to eat for breakfast, what to wear, when we check our phone, who to message, what to pull up or swipe through. For we are creatures of habit and, while at one time we might have given great thought to all the previously mentioned items, we now might regulate them to habit, doing them without even thinking. Most of us don't really think about how to brush our teeth or tie our shoes. Perhaps you have had the experience of driving to work or a friend's house, pulling into a parking space or driveway, and then suddenly becoming aware of having no memory of the trip.

It is interesting how we can do many things without giving them much thought, while at the same time spend immense amount of time, effort, and anxiety making other decisions. For we all know that some decisions will have greater impact on our lives than others and this motivates us to give these decisions more careful consideration.

These leads to a simple and profound question to consider—what are the decisions that come our way that are the most important?

Are these decisions that will impact an important relationship? Are these monetary decisions? Are these decisions that speak to a person's character? Are these decisions where there is no easy right answer or where the wrong decision could result in unpleasant consequences?

It is very human to postpone unpleasant decisions or those that don't seem time sensitive. Many of us are choice adverse, and given the myriad of possibilities, this may seem counterintuitive. With so many possibilities, clearly one option would seem so obvious, but it is almost the opposite. When you are faced with only three flavors of ice cream to choose from, the answer seems so much easier than when you have fifty flavors to choose from. Also, because information is so widely available, you might tend to keep gathering options, reviews, and information before you decide. If the decision is important, we might slip into a sort of information paralysis and postpone any decision. That path might seem easier, but no decision is also a decision, for life will continue and the opportunity may evaporate.

Remember when you began at college. Freshman orientation was a time when everything seemed new and strange, but from the beginning, we pushed you to reflect and choose. Now, you are practiced at decision-making. This is one of the skills we required you to demonstrate multiple times prior to graduation. We required you to make decisions about what courses to take; what themes and concepts to use and apply in papers, projects, and presentations; what friendships to make; where to live; and, of course, what major and occupation to pursue.

In college you made so many life-altering decisions, weighing multiple options. It really is one of the most transformative times in a person's life, making choices that are foundational, leading to lifelong friendships, areas of interest, an understanding of self with likes and dislikes, and the identification of possible jobs and careers.

In school or at work, you are forced to make decisions to meet deadlines and stay on target—but in other parts of life there is no one assigning you a task to complete. How do we handle the responsibility of making all the decisions that are required year after year? One common way in which we handle the responsibility for setting priorities and making decisions within our daily lives is by making lists.

We live in a world of lists. For example, there are to-do lists, lists of the top five things to do, or bucket lists. You name it and there is a list.

Make a list of your priorities; list out what you really want to achieve. Prioritize it. Weigh it out with pluses or minuses. Make a to do list, and put the most important item at the top.

We all make lists. I do this as well, I make many lists, but I should, for full disclosure, share with you that I am not very good at following the lists I make. However, the simple task of making a to-do list lets me keep a few of the items that are flowing through my mind contained, rather than constantly using up my mental energy.

When making a to-do list, most of us realize at the outset, when our pencil is still making the list, that lists have limitations. The list is never completed. It is always evolving, being added to. It is organic and fluid. Items will not be completed in the sequence on the list from one to two to three, from the top of the list to the bottom. You must give the list flexibility.

The completion of some items on this list provides a sense of great joy and a feeling of accomplishment; others provide little solace. For example, you did all the laundry and now you can mark that off your list. You feel some sense of accomplishment, but it is a fleeting feeling because you realize quite quickly that the pile of dirty clothes begins again that night. In fact, your joy can soon turn to frustration and disillusionment.

Perhaps, this is because many of the items that are important in our lives never fully (or ever) appear on one of our lists. So, instead of writing down another to-do list, project list, grocery list, or Christmas list, perhaps it is time to author some other type of list, one that helps us organize and reflect upon the bigger picture and more transformative choices, decisions, and actions.

For example, a "wonder list." This is the list that contains the places you want to go and the things you want to experience. The list that contains all those things that can change your perspective about life and the world or cause you to be self-reflective or grow and rekindle that sense of wonderment. Some people call it their bucket list.

Similarly, what about a "make-a-difference list"? This is the list that contains all the simple actions you will take that will make a difference in the world, like recycling, or contacting a friend you haven't heard from in forever. The list can also include a commitment to donate time or money to a cause that is important to you.

There is also the "legacy list." This is the list of all lists. It doesn't need to be written in erasable ink, but it contains what might be the most important items in your life. For example, what do you want to be known for having done in your life? How about how you have treated others or how you have spent that greatest of resources, time? It might also include what gifts you want to leave to the next generation.

Among the many choices and decisions we make each day and throughout the years are those that deal with daily life and those that affect us, those around us, and the world in more profound and critical ways.

How do you handle your responsibility to your community, to the earth, and to those who are struggling in our society? The world is always moving on, so as a learning being, what do you need or want to learn? How do you want to be seen by others? What will be your legacy? What footprint will you leave?

If you've ever hiked in a national park, you know at the trailhead there will often be signs that say, "Pack out what you take in" and "Leave the park better than you found it." Both messages are designed to make you aware of the impact your choices make on the environment. But what if those signs were applied to everyday life? Leave the world better than you found it. Better for the planet, better for society, better for the community, and better for the next generation. It all comes down to the choices we make.

QUESTIONS FOR SELF-REFLECTION

1. What are the most important and pressing decisions to make in your life right now?
2. What lists do you currently make? Are there some changes to consider in how you make and use your lists?
3. What would be on your wonder list or make-a-difference list?

Chapter 13

Why Diversity Matters

Dr. Robert A. Scott, president emeritus, Adelphi University

College graduates, whether they are Asian, Black, Latino, Native American, other Indigenous, or white, will live in communities and work in enterprises that are influenced by international and intercultural endeavors. They will be neighbors of, supervise, or be supervised by persons of a different ethnicity, nationality, race, gender, or religion. Therefore, it is imperative for colleges to create diverse communities of students, faculty, and staff. The high schools and towns from which higher education institutions recruit students do not provide this diversity; colleges must shape it, because experience with diversity promotes learning.

The philosophical basis for respecting diversity is that it is the "fair" or ethical and equitable thing to do. It is ethical to honor individual differences and treat people equitably. Beyond ethics, it is the law. There are federal, state, and local laws that prohibit discrimination and require remedies for past acts of discrimination.

Beyond the law, though, there are pragmatic reasons for fostering diversity. It makes good sense to cast a wide net in searching for talent, especially when we look at trends in population statistics. If we don't look widely and consider diverse populations, we will limit the capabilities of our organizations. After all, which is more important: preserving a traditional view of who can contribute to achieving the goals or succeeding at accomplishing those goals?

Wise employers attempt a "futures" perspective. They know that a good record in managing diversity now, in recruitment, retention, and advancement, will give them a competitive advantage in recruiting from among an increasingly diverse society in the future. They know that individual and group success requires teamwork, and that teamwork requires respect for others. In addition, these employers expect that they will have managers who are better attuned to the increasing diversity of customers, not only in the U.S. but in other countries as well.

Our institutions must respect diversity as a goal. By this, I mean not only seeking "representation" and providing "support" but a true multiculturalism in which diversity is sought and celebrated. To do this successfully, we honor what we each have in common with others as well as what we each can contribute to the community in distinct and unique ways.

In years past, families of means sponsored their children to study in other countries, travel widely, learn another language, and become familiar with cultures other than their own. Why? Because it is valuable to have experiences beyond the local. Today, just as we think a much larger proportion of youth should attend college, we believe that all students should experience a variety of cultures to better prepare them for work and citizenship in a diverse world.

Diversity is not only a means for expanding one's horizons; it is a means for exploding group stereotypes. A diverse community helps us consider individuals and their unique talents as distinct from their backgrounds and group affiliation. The university president who said to me that 7 percent of his students were "diverse" misunderstood the notion of diversity and limited its meaning to African American and Latino students. This is not enough. Diversity has a broader reach.

In contrast to what some say, goals for diversity are not in conflict with aspirations for academic excellence. Most colleges attempt to compose their undergraduate enrollment by giving preference to some students because of particular talents, geographic origin, or parental affiliation with the institution, in addition to academic preparation. It is in this spirit that we seek to nurture the diversity of the student body, enhance the diversity of the faculty and staff, and celebrate the diversity of alumni and friends. We do it because it matters.

As you will learn, diversity issues go beyond who is taught. They are related to "who" teaches and "what" is to be taught; what students need to know as well as what students want to study. Diversity relates to faculty research and public service as well as to instruction, campus governance, and areas of administration and general education.

Issues of diversity can and should give attention to student clubs and activities, staffing decisions, trustee appointments, student enrollment targets, partnerships with schools and corporations, even outreach programs to the community as well as the curriculum and faculty. In these activities and more, we can and must help you, our students, prepare for citizenship and careers in an increasingly interdependent and multicultural world. We are interdependent economically, environmentally, and militarily, if not always philosophically.

In considering the topic of diversity, we should remember the admonition to think globally, because diversity means different things in different cultures. While we in the United States might be concerned about "white privilege," we need to understand it in relation to dynamics in other countries, including those with concerns about caste systems, Aborigines, and First Peoples. In our own state of Hawaii, white people are the ones viewed as different.

Diversity is "a matter of color, texture, and size, as in a quilt." Thus said Jesse Jackson, activist and former U. S. presidential candidate. He described diversity as consisting of "many patches, many pieces, many colors, many sized, all woven and held together by a common thread."' And Shirley Chisholm, former member of the U.S. House of Representatives, said, "We Americans have a chance to become someday a nation in which all racial stocks and classes can exist in their own selfhoods but meet on a basis of respect and quality and live together socially, canonically, and politically."

To enhance campus culture, improve student retention, and further institutional development, we need to have a comprehensive strategy for diversity development for the benefit of all students. This is our commitment and students have a role in it.

Communications, technologies, and transportation make it possible for multiple cultures to exist side by side. Diversity of age, gender, race, nationality, ethnicity, religion, and socioeconomic background is essential. If we are to prepare students for careers and citizenship, and help our school, community, and business partners achieve success, then we must be committed to an education that considers all the dimensions of diversity.

QUESTIONS FOR REFLECTION

1. Have you lived in a community or attended a school with a diversity of cultures represented? How did that influence your perspective?
2. Which dimensions of diversity are of greatest interest to you?
3. People are sometimes uncomfortable in a diverse setting. How would you advise them?

Chapter 14

What You Say Matters

Dr. Drew Bogner, president
emeritus, Molloy University

For many years while president, I taught the History of Modern Japan. The course was connected to the college's Study Abroad Program, and I served as a content expert on four student trips to Japan. Some were in the summer, others in January during intersession. On one January trip we traveled to Mount Koya and stayed for a night at a Buddhist monastery. It was cold with snow on the ground, and the only source of heat in our shoji paper–doored rooms was an electric blanket of sorts. That evening we gathered in a common room to hear a presentation by the head monk. He apologized for the cold, noting that one of the heaters was not working. Behind him was a screen on which he displayed various images. The room was dark except for the light from the projector, and in the cold I could see his breath in its light.

He spoke about the power of words, for words carry intent. "If you speak harshly to a plant," he said, "it will not grow as well. However, if you speak more lovingly it will thrive. 'What a lovely plant you are, so beautiful,' rather than, 'You are a sad and dreadful plant. If you do not grow, I think I will have to throw you away.'" The same can be said of water, he explained, and showed photos of water droplets taken through a microscope. The water that had been exposed to positive language had a regular, symmetrical, crystalline structure or pattern. Conversely, the ice of the water that had been exposed to harsh language had an irregular pattern.

I cannot say how scientifically valid the evidence is of the influence of words on plants or water, but from my own experience there is truth to the fact that words matter. Words can, when uttered, serve like violent projectiles that penetrate another to their very soul. What we say and how we say it can change the whole tenor of a room. Our words can also be a soothing balm to another, elicit laughter, and show that we care.

One year as part of the Joseph Maher Leadership Forum, Molloy College was fortunate to have on campus Mr. Paul Rusesabagina, whose heroic acts inspired the movie *Hotel Rwanda*. In 1994, Mr. Rusesabagina was the manager of a luxury hotel in Rwanda. When terrorism and mass executions engulfed the whole country, leading to the deaths of 800,000 people in a span of one hundred days, Mr. Rusesabagina was able to shelter 1,268 people inside the hotel, saving them from almost certain murder.

Afterward, he attempted to come to some understanding of how his neighbors and countrymen could turn on each other, brandishing machetes to brutally maim and kill the person across the street or mere children. Looking back on his own situation, he attempted to understand as well, how he, an ordinary man, was able to hold back the tidal wave of brutality to save over twelve hundred people.

The answer to both, Mr. Rusesabagina observed, was contained in the power of words. Words of anger, words of prejudice, and words of hatred were used by the newly empowered ruling group to fan old resentments between Hutus and Tutsis.

"The words put out by radio station announcers were a major cause of violence," he said. "They were explicit exhortations for ordinary citizens to break into homes of their neighbors and kill them. . . . The avalanche of words celebrating racial supremacy and encouraging people to do their duty created an alternate reality . . . where the insane was made to seem normal."

Conversely, Mr. Rusesabagina was convinced that the only thing that saved those 1,268 people in the hotel was words—not liquor, not money, not the UN—just ordinary words directed against the darkness.

Words are powerful. We know this from our own experience. There are hurtful words, for example, words of hate, demeaning words, words that divide, and words that twist and bend the truth. However, there are also words of good, words that enliven, words that calm, words that connect and bind, bridging divides and building up rather than tearing down.

The words we use in conversation can have a real effect on others, but so too are the words we put into text. In fact, these words can have even more impact, for these words have a staying power. There is a visible record of them that can be looked at time and time again or forwarded and shown to others. What we type in a moment of anger can have a lasting effect, exhibiting a life well after our anger has subsided.

We each hold power in the words we use. We are all consumers and practitioners of word usage and know their impact on others and on ourselves. We know each of us will be viewed and judged by what we say and how we say it. As such, we are called to be stewards of words, giving conscious thought to the words we choose to use before we utter them and inject them into a conversation.

In the years you have spent in college you have read many words, spoken many words, and come to understand words in clear and more profound ways. How will you use this newfound knowledge? How will you use your newfound vocabulary? How will you use your words?

Will you use your words for good? Will you say or allow another to say some words repeatedly to distort the truth and demean others?

One word, one single word or one short phrase, can elicit a whole range of thoughts and emotions. In this way both the monk and Mr. Rusesabagina were right. If you say, "I love you" or "I respect you" to someone, it is incredibly powerful and changes how the other person will respond back to you. There are also words chosen to wound others, or tear them down, or belittle them.

In an ironic sort of way, we can become known as a certain type of person by the words we choose to say and when and how we say them. You can be known as a person who is funny or boring or insightful or caustic. You can become labeled as a person who is caring or mean and hateful, not because of your actions but because of what you said.

Words are indeed powerful. Individual words and phrases can elicit action in others, and you bear some responsibility for how the other person reacts to what you say. Just think what the world would be like if people gave more thought to what they might say before they said it. You cannot control much of life, but you can control what you say, when you say it, and how you say it. What you say really matters.

QUESTIONS FOR REFLECTION

1. What are some examples in your life when your communications have influenced the actions of others in positive or negative ways?
2. How will you choose your words more carefully in the future?
3. Given the power you have in the words you choose to use, where might you use your words to elicit positive change?
4. Given the power you have in the words you choose to use, how might you respond constructively to someone who says something negative to you?

Chapter 15

Being an Effective Leader

Dr. Drew Bogner, president emeritus, Molloy University

The year was 1862, and Abraham Lincoln was faced with a decision. Preparations for the war were running far below expectations. There were numerous charges of graft and corruption—insider deals. Accounting was bad. Simon Cameron, who Lincoln had placed in office as secretary of war to consolidate his power in Pennsylvania, was not doing the job. Lincoln had no choice. He removed Cameron and replaced him with Edwin Stanton, a staunch critic of Lincoln's own policies and a man who had once humiliated Lincoln in a trial in Cincinnati. The move was risky politically, but within one year production was exceeding expectations and Stanton had become one of Lincoln's most loyal supporters. Without Stanton, the war might have been lost.

In 1940, Britain was locked in a life-or-death struggle with Nazi Germany. Franklin Roosevelt, president of the United States, was acutely aware that without the proper armaments and supplies Britain could not hold out long against the Germans. He knew that America must supply Britain with armaments. However, America had a long tradition of isolationism, and legislation in effect at the time prohibited the U.S. from selling weapons to another country without congressional approval. For many weeks FDR ruminated over the dilemma, and then one evening he suddenly came up with an idea, later termed "lend-lease": the U.S. would lend the weapons to Britain, and at the end of the war Britain would repay the U.S., not in money but in kind, replacing the weapons lost.

On September 11, 2001, Sandler O'Neill, a modest-sized bond trading firm located on the 104th floor of 2 World Trade Center, was devastated by the loss of 66 of its 177 employees. Jimmy Dunne was the one surviving partner. He had been playing golf that day at a charity tournament in upstate New York. Faced with possible financial ruin and still grieving the loss of his best friends and business partners, he made a courageous decision. Sandler O'Neill would continue to pay salaries to all employees, including the families of those employees who had been killed in the attack. Making a commitment as senior management to attend all memorial services and deal with the bereavement as a top priority, the company also announced that it would reopen for business on September 17. Impressed by the courage of the company, Sandler O'Neill's competitors provided them with space to reopen the business and cut them in on business deals.

Though separated by 150 years with varying technologies and cultural differences, all three examples demonstrate some of the fundamental aspects of leadership. All three leaders, Lincoln, Roosevelt, and Dunne, were visionary and unconventional in their solution to a problem. Each was motivated to act out of commitment to a higher or greater purpose. Each demonstrated integrity of character and willingness to take a risk to accomplish an important goal.

Many of the essential characteristics of leadership are timeless. Drawing on more than four hundred case studies and exhaustive surveys of thousands of people spanning research over twenty years, Jim Kouzes and Barry Posner[1] found a remarkable consistency in the characteristics people value in admired leaders. The four traits that are consistently listed above all others are honesty, the ability to be forward looking, inspiration, and competency. To use other language, we expect leaders to be visionary, have integrity, and be competent.

The value-based characteristics that allow one to demonstrate integrity and honesty, walk the talk, and display courage do not depend as much on the particulars of time and society. However, the other essential characteristics of leadership, such as competency and being visionary or forward looking, are influenced directly by the signs of the times.

Clearly if we value competency in a leader, that leader must continue to renew their knowledge base, staying up to date on trends, technologies, and ways of doing business.

To construct a compelling vision, the leader must be attuned to current trends and future possibilities. Seeing the world as it once was or only as it is today is not enough for the leader, and no compelling vision can come from only looking to the past or keeping things the way they are now.

Many great leaders are masters of communication, both mastering the technology of the day but also understanding their audience so that they can connect the message in a compelling way to them. Lincoln was a master storyteller in a time when the oral word was the main means of communication. FDR mastered the new medium of radio with his fireside chats. A leader must master the communication tools and medium of the day.

Kouzes and Posner maintain that a leader must be good and adept at five things:

1. Challenging the process
2. Inspiring a shared vision
3. Enabling others to act
4. Modeling the way
5. Encouraging the heart

CHALLENGING THE PROCESS

An essential characteristic of a leader is their ability to see possibilities, search them out, and find opportunities to construct a compelling vision. The universe has expanded, and the pace of change has accelerated, such that the process of change is not linear but multifaceted and more complex. This necessitates, in the leader, a wider scope of visioning that requires incorporating many viewpoints. Forecasting is harder. Gone is the five-year plan, and in its place is the three-month trend analysis.

Leaders must be able to tolerate a higher level of risk. Leaders must also be adept at using a multifaceted approach to make changes, moving forward on many fronts, being willing to drop one idea to pursue another, moving sideways. Because of the interconnectedness of the world, a leader must be willing to develop partnerships with others including with those who would have traditionally been viewed as competitors or previously seen as unaligned entities.

INSPIRING A SHARED VISION

The concept that vision-making within an organization is the sole purview of the CEO or senior manager is rapidly being challenged. In many industries the vision, is increasingly borne out of the work of many. What CEO can really keep up with everything that is going on in the global and regional markets or within a given industry?

Nurturing and communicating the vision is extremely important. The leader must be able to harness the varied communication strategies that exist within an institution. One must be attuned to the speed at which rumor and half-truths can flow through an organization and cripple a vision. A vision is only effective if it is understood and accepted as relevant,

ENABLING OTHERS TO ACT

A good leader understands that the vision becomes a reality only through the actions of others and that part of being an effective leader is finding ways to enable others to act. The first step in empowering and enabling others is to set clear goals, objectives, and measures, making sure that people are clear on what is expected, why it is important, and how it all fits together into a broader vision.

Providing the necessary resources of business is another major component of this. These resources include technology and equipment but also the training and workforce to complete various tasks and achieve goals.

MODELING THE WAY

This is walking the talk and doing what you say you will do. The constant of integrity is extremely important, but so is the need to be credible. To be credible, a leader must stay up to date on trends and be informed. This makes it essential that we are information consumers and futurists.

Not only is there just-in-time manufacturing, but we also live in world of just-in-time management. We make a hundred decisions a day. We receive hundreds of emails and texts a day, and there is a real expectation that these are answered almost immediately. We are driven to manage in real time, in the now, with little time for reflection.

As perceived visionaries, it is incumbent upon us that we find a way to slow down real-time management so that good decisions can be made, particularly decisions that are consistent with a high moral value framework. Remember, leaders will be judged as much on integrity as on competency.

ENCOURAGING THE HEART

This is the art of rewarding and celebrating accomplishments, as well as building morale. There is an increased desire and expectation among workers that their place of employment and their managers value their contributions and recognize their accomplishments and efforts, treating them as individuals. It is not coincidence that these workplaces have more satisfied employees who are more productive and wish to stay. As such, attending to the culture of the organization and to developing and executing a plan that attends to the human side of the workplace is increasingly essential.

Leaders must have increasing higher levels of EQ (emotional intelligence), noting the possible perceptions that a varied audience might have to language and various actions.

One of the dangers of our digital interconnectedness is the possible removal of face-to-face interactions. One of the lessons of the COVID-19 pandemic is that it is important for a leader to be conscious of this danger. Remember, a good leader attends to the humanity of their coworkers.

A good leader is called to be both visionary and competent, to have integrity and walk the talk. Some traits such as honesty and integrity are based on strong moral positions and value systems and, as such, are more timeless. Others such as competency and the ability to be visionary are directly dependent on the whirlwinds of social, cultural, and technological changes swirling around us.

In the end, though, it is the leader who must determine which of these social, cultural, and technological forces have real impact. It is the leader, as Max De Pree states, who ultimately must define reality.

Here's to the future. It awaits those who have the courage, ability, and heart to lead.

QUESTIONS FOR REFLECTION

1. What leadership roles have you held in the past?
2. How did you inspire others to act, and how did you model the behavior you wanted others to display?
3. Is there some opportunity for leadership that you are presently considering? What are the skills that you would bring to it?

NOTE

1. Kouzes, James M., and Posner, Barry Z. *The Leadership Challenge.* 3rd ed. San Francisco: Jossey-Bass, 2002.

Chapter 16

Developing Leadership Skills

Dr. Robert A. Scott, president emeritus, Adelphi University

There are many theories of leadership and stories about leaders. One of the frequent lessons cited is the importance of listening—being aware with eyes as well as with ears. Listening is key to critical analysis, the skills and ability necessary to identify a problem, the first step in solving or addressing it. At times it means reflecting on a proposal and saying, "That's a solution; what's the problem?"

Other lessons about effective leadership recommend reading in order to refine the use of language as well as to expand our knowledge and understanding; speaking in formal as well as in informal settings and using these occasions to remind others about an institution's mission and purpose; writing notes of congratulations and condolence as well as essays and speeches promoting educational values; reflecting on the purpose of life as well as on what we can learn from an experience; showing empathy, that is, attempting to understand the feelings and fears of others; and appreciating the importance of context, the circumstances in which leadership is required.

One of the more insightful comments on the topic of leadership was attributed to Freddie Mercury in the film *Bohemian Rhapsody*, the story of Freddie and the band Queen. The scene is in their lawyer's office and Freddie is asking to rejoin the group to perform at Live Aid in Wimbledon. One of his bandmates, still stung by Freddie's departure from the group after being offered a large recording contract, challenges him by saying, "You have your own band now. Why do you need us?" Freddie replies, "Yes, I have my own band and more money, but it is not the same. They do everything I tell them, and that is the problem. They do not challenge me to be better, the way you did."

Whether fact or fiction, the scene demonstrates vividly that leadership requires integrity, humility, and reflection, the recognition that a leader cannot act alone and be most effective. Unfortunately, there are too many examples of those in leadership positions who demand fealty instead of welcoming pushback. An effective team is one in which the whole is greater than the sum of the parts. Such teams require trust, not loyalty oaths and secrets. They know that sharing information builds alliances and that control of data threatens trust.

Another trait of some in leadership positions is to act as if the history of the organization started on the day they took office. To paraphrase an old quote, institutions are the lengthened shadow of past leaders. Institutional history and heritage are essential starting points for continuity as well as change. The values of the founders should undergird the vision of the future.

A variant of this style is found in leaders who decide that they want "their own" team and either remove or force out members of the inherited senior administration before even knowing the culture of the institution. Not only does this ignore the importance of institutional memory, but it also can destabilize long-term external as well as internal relationships.

This pattern was more common in corporations than in colleges and universities, but as corporate executives have become more prominent on institutional boards, the practice has grown in higher education as well. While the board should not prohibit such changes, it should give guidance to the new leader, especially if there was an inside candidate for the post. After all, the board's role is to protect the institution of the future from the actions of the present.

Another pattern borrowed from business is the "CEO" president, that is, one who fulfills the meaning of this title by focusing on scale, delegation, money, and markets while giving only lip service to mission. One consequence of this is that a president can talk about "shared governance" with faculty but treat them as employees rather than as partners in governing the institution. I prefer the CMO (chief mission officer) model of leadership; he or she must mind the money, of course, but demonstrate real shared governance.

Listening, analyzing, reading, speaking, writing, empathy, context or circumstance, and reflection are essential dimensions of leadership. The greatest of these is the self-awareness that comes from reflection, of listening and analyzing. And reflection comes from a liberal education, whether undertaken as a literature major or as an accounting major taking general education courses.

To prepare students for lives of leadership, we in the faculty and administration must reflect on what colleges should teach and what students should study. That is, we should ask about the areas of knowledge, both general and expert; skills, such as writing and speaking with grace and persuasion;

abilities, such as analysis and leadership; and values, such as teamwork and respect for others, that a college graduate should possess.

One way to consider this question is to reflect on contemporary crises in finance, industry, and politics, and ask what lessons have been learned. A quick survey of even the recent past suggests that too many people, even those in highly responsible roles, lacked knowledge of history or the tools of historical analysis, and had neither the personal nor professional memory in which to place contemporary issues.

History, then, is an essential subject, especially if we are to understand the different ways people "know" the truth and how they challenge assumptions and validate assertions. In the study of history as defined here, we learn about the world we meet (nature or science); the world we make (culture); and the systems by which we mediate between them (law, morality, ethics, and religion). We learn about the past and present, science and technology, war and peace, poetry and prose. We learn how we know what we think we know by learning to distinguish between empirical evidence, epiphanies or faith, and emotions based in fear or superstition.

The study of history helps us learn what it means to focus on what is important and cultivates our sensibilities. It helps us think in terms of time, to understand how society has changed and continues to change, to consider an institution's or a community's heritage, and to wonder how the founders imagined different futures for themselves and others.

The second area to develop is that of imagination. It seems clear when thinking about recent challenges that even corporate and political leaders confronted new problems without the ability to see connections among different variables, visualize or forecast directions, or consider unintended consequences. They had not developed the capacity to inquire, to experience discovery, to wonder and ask. These are the benefits of an education that liberates students from prejudices masquerading as principles, no matter what their degree program or ethnicity, nationality, socioeconomic status, or age. Students need to develop a global perspective and foster inclusive communities even as they live, work, and volunteer locally.

The third area for leaders to develop and exhibit is that of compassion. Many articles about leadership mention empathy as necessary to lead others. While this is true, as noted earlier, a leader should also develop the capacity for compassion. If we move beyond sympathy (feeling sorry for another) and develop empathy (appreciating the pain or condition of another), then we can learn compassion, the ability to turn empathy into socially responsible actions in service to others. This, too, is part of higher education's mission to prepare active citizens and professionals—and leaders.

The fourth area is that of reflection, the habit of considering what the experience or incident means to us. It the habit of mind to ponder on what is going right and why, as well as on what is not going well and why. It is the necessary ability to identify the problem to be solved before attempting to solve it. This does not mean we engage in what some call "paralysis by analysis." It means that we to ask, "What is this? What can I learn from this?" It is the method by which we seek to understand the challenges before us and meaning in our lives.

Taken together, understanding what came before, imagining new perspectives, serving others, and taking the time to reflect on the issue or challenge, purpose and meaning, form the basis of effective leadership. A transformational leader knows not only how to analyze and solve problems, but also how to identify which problems to solve.[1]

QUESTIONS FOR REFLECTION

1. Whose leadership style do you admire? Why?
2. What are several characteristics of leadership that you want to emulate?
3. Describe an incident in which you expressed empathy or compassion.

NOTE

1. A version of this chapter appeared as "Leaders, Listening, and Liberal Education," *Liberal Education*, Fall 2022.

Chapter 17

Finding and Feeding Your Creativity

Dr. Drew Bogner, president emeritus, Molloy University

Around a decade ago I traveled to southern Spain with my wife, Karen, and our two children, who were in college at the time. Now that they were adults, I wanted to involve them in the decision-making for the trip, deciding where we should go and what we might see, so I handed them the guidebook and asked them to scope out an itinerary for the day.

They came back with a suggestion that we visit two venues, both described in the book in two simple sentences. The first was the site of an obscure Roman ruin, located in a farmer's field, really a series of unexcavated piles of stones and brush except for a well-preserved and excavated amphitheater.

The second venue took us along a rural highway, skirting a muddy river, to a simple sign that announced Cueva de la Pileta. There wasn't much to the place, a small gravel parking lot and kiosk with a vine-covered arbor with refreshments for sale. We paid a small fee, and we were led with a handful of others to a thick wooden door in the side of the hill. Our guide produced a large iron key from his pocket and unlocked the door, ushering us in. He lit two gas lanterns, closed and locked the door, and led us into the cavern.

As we walked deeper into the cave, the images began to appear, cave paintings from twenty-five thousand years ago, of horses, elk, deer in red ocher and black charcoal, the creative work of human beings who lived in an entirely different world than ours. These images of interpreted reality were laid down in a time and place quite different from today but speaking all the same to me, through my own consciousness, giving me a new understanding of my own sense of time and place.

It was one of the most powerful encounters of my life and quite happenstance in how it came about. It left me with two thoughts, two insights that I took away that day. First is the understanding that at our heart we are creative beings. We have a curiosity about our reality and a need to make it personal—to interpret it, to own it, to make sense of it, and to communicate it.

Second, that interpretation is so fundamental to human nature that it transcends both the time of modern human existence and variety of culture and place. Dimensional art leaves a physical trace, and so it is hard to deny that it has been important over time to human existence.

I suspect that music, rhythm, and voice are just as central to human existence over time. There is plenty of evidence of ancient instruments from physical artifacts found in tombs and burial vaults and reference to song in many ancient texts.

It is not hard to imagine that concomitant with the development of language and the need to express ourselves, "word" utterances of communication were put into a rhythmic pattern of song. Some ancient languages include whistle vocalizations, more effective in communicating over large distances.

We find as human beings every possible way of expressing ourselves with music. In Edinburgh, while traveling, I listened to a performer playing a saw with a bow, and in Quebec City, an artist evoking music from the rim of water goblets. Then there is my good friend who taps his class ring rhythmically on the steering wheel to the beat of music almost unconsciously as he drives.

Art and music are some of the most natural expressions of being. Why do we love to dance, and why is it so prevalent? This almost inability to sit still in the face of rhythm and melody. What does a three-year-old do at an outdoor concert? Get up and move and dance.

The arts are essential to being human. This is why we see them throughout the ages of development from the beginning to the end of life. The arts can evoke powerful emotions stirring memories of place and time. A photograph can elicit a mood of tranquility, a yearning, a sense of being or, conversely, present in a disturbing way a challenge to our sense of right and wrong or injustice.

When I had the opportunity a couple of years ago to see an exhibit of *National Geographic* women photographers in DC, I was swept away by the range of emotions that I experienced and the conversations that were elicited in me about how I viewed the world and myself in it.

The same can be said for a personal encounter with a painting. *The Scream* by Edvard Munch, seen in person, is disturbing—and rightly so—as an expression of the lamentation for modernity. However, when you see it as I did, at an exhibition at MOMA with other versions of this work, you begin to see as well the subtle variations that were in the mind of the artist, reminding us that we see the world in half tones and not in cold, hard, objective, and measurable ways.

Music is equally evocative. We all know this and have experienced the phenomenon of how a particular song can remind us of a single event and usher in feelings of emotions.

I know that I am not alone in how music and art have enriched my life in powerful and meaningful ways, and I am sure that every single one of us can come up with our own list of how music and art influence us on almost a daily basis.

We are at our core creative beings. We are not passive entities that only respond to the outside world in routine, dispassionate ways. We want to make sense of what we see. We want to express ourselves. We want to shape the world. We want to share what we have created with others.

The need to create is deep within our souls, but it is important to understand that being creative is not the same as being artistic. Our creativity is on display every day. It seeps out in how we rearrange and decorate the spaces where we live and work. It appears in the emojis and texts we use to communicate with others. It resonates in the projects we do, the planning, the assembly of materials, in the doing and the satisfaction that follows, whether it is planting a garden, painting a room, or assembling a piece of IKEA furniture.

You might be one of those persons who channels this creative impulse into visual art, into music, or onto the page, journaling or creating poetry, looking for ways to make sense of the world and share these insights with others. I have felt this creative presence in a vivid imagination that has always occupied my mind, but I didn't see myself as particularly creative, because I wasn't an artist or writer, or composer, or any of those things that we label in society as creative.

If I had been asked in high school, in college, or in the years right out of college if I was creative—I would have said I wasn't particularly so. The answer to that question changed as my life unfolded because I came to two powerful observations about creativity.

First, I can understand that being creative is first and foremost a personal thing. We paint, or write, or create visual montages, because it allows us to express what we see and what we feel. We do it, as the artists in the cave did, to make sense of reality and channel it into something that contains our perspective.

So, I decided to journal—not every day but when we traveled. I wrote about what we did, what I saw, and the experiences we had. As I did this, something happened in me. I started to write about how I felt and how the things I saw and experienced affected me. The act of writing gave me the ability to see deeper inside and brought out another side of me.

Chapter 17

I started to write poetry, allowing it to come out as well, in chunks and rifts, but only at the times when I really needed to express how I felt. I started journaling and writing as a way of capturing a record of life with my children, and it evolved into a way of expressing who I was and what I was experiencing in life. The act of doing, of creating, led to my evolution as well, allowing me to see things in ways I never did before.

The same is true of my and Karen's hobby of photography. We look for the hidden perspective, framing the photo in unique ways, waiting for the sun to hit the horizon or the clouds to wander across the sky, or trying to capture the hummingbird or butterfly in midflight, freezing their beating wings.

We have taken tens of thousands of photographs, but outside of one photography exhibition, we have done this just for ourselves. All the acts of creating the perfect shot, from the perfect perspective, this creative endeavor, have changed how I see the world. I now see the detail behind the obvious, the subtle movements of the clouds, and the changing palette of colors that paint the world where we live.

So, the first observation is that we are all creative beings and exhibit this creativity every day. The key to being more creative is to set aside labels and just do. Write, paint, compose, on paper or digitally, just do it. Do it for you; do it when it feels right and when you need to express yourself.

The second observation is that creativity is not limited to a narrow set of artistic endeavors. As you build a career and family, you will find that there is little free time for just you. Time evaporates into work projects, taxi service, yard work, and just keeping up with daily routines. This is the way of life. I came to understand that the expression of my creative self often occurred within these life tasks of career and being a dad.

In my career as an educator, I built courses, designing classroom experiences that brought concepts to life, first in biology labs and later with aspects of Japanese history. Later, it was in the building of academic programs and then designing buildings. More than just a job, these are forms of creative expression if you allow them to be.

Some years ago, I had the privilege of meeting Malcolm Gladwell, the essayist who writes about our uniquely human way of interacting and encountering life. In his book *Outliers*, he attempts to explain why some individuals succeed more than others in a variety of roles. Sometimes it is because of natural talent, in athletics or as a musician or artist, for example. However, in many cases it is because of the ten-thousand-hour rule. People who seem really good at something might make it look easy and natural, but they have spent at least ten thousand hours doing it.

This insight led to a very personal question. What is something I do well that I have spent at least ten thousand hours doing? The answer is communicating, speaking, and talking, in front of people, distilling complexity into consumable and understandable observations, concepts, and ideas. Looking back at my speeches from fifteen or twenty years ago, I can see that I am better now at communicating and better at being a storyteller.

I came to understand that communicating to others, whether as a teacher or a university leader, was the palette that I used to express my creativity. You will find, if you have not already done so, some part of life, some part of your career that will serve as the blank canvas for the expression of your creativity. Embrace it with confidence and see it for what it is: the opportunity to display that most human of characteristics, creativity.

QUESTIONS FOR REFLECTION

1. In what everyday and occasional ways do you display your creativity?
2. Is there an additional medium where you want to be creative?
3. Do you want to make this a priority? If so, how will you find time to do so?

Chapter 18

Finding the Job of the Future

Dr. Drew Bogner, president emeritus, Molloy University

How do you prepare for a world that does not exist now, and how do you prepare for a job or a career in that future world?

These questions are ones that higher education is asking itself daily. In many ways we generally know the answers to these questions. There is great unanimity among employers as to what are the fundamental skills, attributes, and characteristics that they are looking for in an employee. True, the world of work has changed drastically over the past few decades, and the COVID-19 pandemic only served to accelerate this change.

Increasingly, employment opportunities lie in jobs requiring higher levels of social and analytical skills. Coincidently, employment is rising faster in jobs that call for greater preparation, education, or experience and training. The pandemic accelerated the trends toward remote work, e-commerce, and automation. The gig economy, already growing throughout the twenty-first century, has accelerated as well, with a real acceptance and dependence on independent contractors.

So what are the fundamental skills, attributes, and characteristics that employers want in their employees? Communication skills top the list. This includes writing in numerous formats from short and succinct to longer and more complex, oral communication, and presentation skills. Employers want individuals who can analyze, problem solve, and make critical decisions based on data. Information literacy is the gold standard, the ability to find information, validate information, and apply it in planning and problem solving. There is an increasing level of digital literacy that is expected as well, knowing how to use technology in a workplace setting.

Many employers want individuals with business acumen. This translates to mastering tasks that are common in most organizations, including strategic planning, data collection and analysis, assessment, development of guidelines and protocols, and budget management. More recently added to the list are cultural knowledge and the ability to work with people of varying backgrounds and cultures, a diversity intelligence. If you can speak another language, this is a real plus. Lastly, since the world of work is changing rapidly and jobs are constantly being reconstructed, learning skills are highly valued. This means a willingness to be constantly learning and the ability to learn on your own.

In addition to these skills and abilities are what we would call the "soft" skills and, despite what the name might imply, these are just as important to employers. These include interpersonal skills, like how to get along with others. It includes leadership and team member skills. So much can go awry with employees who do not possess these skills that employers are increasingly looking for individuals with high EQ (emotional intelligence). EQ is a newer term that encompasses the ability to relate to people, assess social situations, and act appropriately within them. Another more recent term that many employers are using to describe another set of skills is grit. Grit implies that a person will see something through to the end, stick-to-itiveness. Finally, employers want individuals who are adept at time management.

Almost all employers are looking for character attributes such as honesty, integrity, dependability, loyalty, and flexibility. They are looking for individuals who don't need to be told how to act in every situation but who possess an internal ethical compass that guides them.

While a person can and does accumulate these skills through a whole host of life experiences, a college degree has become a sort of shorthand for the accumulation of this comprehensive skill package. That is not by accident as colleges and universities have fashioned a curriculum and a set of cocurricular activities that seek to build these skills and attributes.

All colleges require a set of communication courses, emphasizing both written and oral communication. Many courses require team-driven projects that hone team skills and interpersonal skills and require the development of presentation skills. Information and digital literacy are taught specifically. So too are critical thinking and problem-solving skills, developing in students the ability to apply a number of conceptual frameworks, from the scientific method to historical analysis, to criticism, to cultural analysis to rhetoric, and statistical analysis. There is a reason why almost every college has a similar set of required core courses, from writing to history; to social, biological, and physical sciences; to literature and the arts; to mathematics; and to philosophy.

Outside of the classroom there are opportunities to develop leadership and interpersonal skills, to develop flexibility and time management skills and deepen a person's sense of grit, ethical compass, and appreciation for diversity. Most every college has an ethical code of conduct, and it is expected that students abide by it.

There is a reason why the American university system has developed a rich set of extracurricular activities that support and enhance what happens in the classroom. In many ways these optional activities serve to build the soft skills and character traits that employers most desire and that serve a person well in their own personal lives. Some institutions have instituted an "experiential transcript" that identifies the skills, traits and abilities that have been built into these activities along with the supporting experiential proof. For example, if you want to speak to a skill of working with individuals from different cultures, identifying a global learning experience would make sense, or managing a budget could speak to the role you had as treasurer of student government.

This proof positive approach is just the process that you will need to follow in securing most jobs today. It is important to have a well-tailored résumé and cover letter, so important in a time when 75 percent of jobs will review your initial materials through an ATS (applicant tracking system) where résumés and applications get digitally sorted and ranked using keywords. However, later in the search process you will need to not only indicate what skills you have but also deliver the proof by detailing your past experiences.

Even though a college degree has become a necessary prerequisite for so many jobs, in and of itself, it does not replace the necessary task of engaging in a deep dive about yourself, organizing your past work and college experiences into those employer-demanded categories. Good preparation always favors the few. Knowing what you learned and in what course, what skills you acquired and in what courses and life experiences, and what character attributes you possess along with examples of where you displayed them is the kind of thought exercise to conduct. Put it on paper, not necessarily to hand out to the recruiter but as job interview preparation.

This knowledge of self is always useful, whether it is for that entry-level job or a senior management position. This will always be the best way to secure the jobs of today or the jobs of the future.

QUESTIONS FOR REFLECTION

1. What would be on your experiential transcript? What skills and abilities do these experiences demonstrate?

2. In what ways can you provide proof that you have some expertise or skill in communication, presentation, teamwork, leadership, and time management?
3. How can you demonstrate that you can work flexibly and independently?

Chapter 19

Prepared for Work, Not Just a Job

Dr. Robert A. Scott, president emeritus, Adelphi University

More than 6.5 percent of people in the world of working age and looking for a job are unemployed. In the U.S., corporations are cutting jobs by the tens of thousands. Throughout the world, there is a relationship between technological innovation and increased unemployment.

How can we break the cycle of unemployment and poverty? Through education!

It is important to remember that technology takes with one hand but gives with another. In 1900, farm employment accounted for nearly 40 percent of all jobs. Today it is about 10 percent. At the conclusion of World War II, service industries accounted for 10 percent of nonfarm employment, compared with 38 percent for manufacturing. Since the 1970s, the American economy has moved away from producing goods to providing services, and the service-producing sector has accounted for an increasing proportion of workers.

In 1970, there were 48.8 million service-providing workers, and 22.2 million people in the goods-producing sector, representing a service-to-goods ratio of 2.2 to 1. By 2000, the number of workers in the service-providing sector was 107.1 million, compared with 24.6 million in the goods-producing sector, representing a service-to-goods ratio of 4.4 to 1. In 2005, according to preliminary statistics compiled by the Bureau of Labor Statistics and published in *Establishment Data Historical Employment* (2005), workers who provided services (111.5 million) outnumbered workers who produced goods (22.1 million) by a ratio of 5 to 1.

What happened to the people displaced? A great many lost jobs but found work.

Jobs as we know them are only about 150 years old. Moreover, corporate employment, the subject of all the stories about downsizing, is only 100 years old, a mere blip in the history of work.

When I was in college, the wealthy kids didn't worry about jobs; they thought about work. My father, with a basic education, urged me to take a salaried job in appliance sales for General Electric. At the same time, some of my college friends were talking about where they should apply their knowledge, skills, abilities, and values—that is, where they would solve problems. And that was the difference. The GE job was an honorable choice, but it was not at a level of problem solving that I aspired to or had been educated for.

As Bill Gates, cofounder of Microsoft, says, jobs are eliminated but "work" or opportunities for problem solving expand. Therefore, we educators must consider how best to prepare students for a future in which they must view themselves as problem solvers in constantly evolving settings for work. How can we prepare for the future?

Education must contribute to the making of a civil society. Cyberwork is both "connecting"—think of the internet and social media—and "disconnecting"—leaving us alone. We must help students find common ground and realize the communal destiny worth striving for.

How do we prepare students for a multicultural, civil America, in which a future Alex Haley could write about the heritage of both his African mother and his Irish father? By fostering multicultural communities of mutual respect.

Throughout the world, educators and public policy groups are trying to determine how best to provide access to collegiate success for students previously excluded from higher education. In Europe, Asia, and South Africa, groups are looking at our opportunity programs trying to determine what works best and what should be changed.

They are looking at philosophical approaches, such as my four essential "I's" (inquisitiveness, interdisciplinarity, involvement, and independence), as well as at practical strategies (students should have the daily discipline to read a national newspaper, study, and exercise).

We know the skills and abilities that organizations desire in employees. Beyond technological know-how and an attitude of continuous learning, employers want people with initiative, creativity, productivity, courage, a willingness to listen, an ability to tolerate ambiguity, interpersonal skills, and the abilities to motivate others, build teamwork, and achieve consensus.

Moreover, it is highly likely that you will work with, do business with, or live among people of a different ethnic, national, or religious background. Therefore, the mission of every college or university should be to advance students' ability to deal with this new world.

We seek to engage students in their studies, to assist in their transformation, not simply to encounter them in a series of transactions as we "deliver" instruction. Cooperative education, internships, and service learning as well as continual professional development for teachers and faculty all reinforce what we do in the classroom.

Seneca said, "The fates guide those who go willingly; those who do not, they drag." The fates seem to say that mobilizing a multicultural and technological society is a must. We need to understand the interplay of teamwork and independence; we need think about work, not just talk about jobs.

Just think of the work to be done in a society: prenatal care; childcare; learning how people learn; tutoring; creating a society that can be free of disease, ignorance, and violence; hospice care; creating communities of common interest; firefighting and ambulance attendants (now largely volunteer efforts); smart roads; sturdy bridges; and much, more.

The work necessary for sustainable, civil communities exists and will continue to expand. Technological tools are increasingly available. Health care coverage can be provided as a "portable" benefit. Are we prepared for such a future? Can we influence higher education and the state and our country in ways that will support this quest? Do we have a choice?

QUESTIONS FOR REFLECTION

1. What is the difference between a job and work?
2. What is the meaning of the saying "I never had a job and never worked a day in my life"?
3. If you were an educator, how would you prepare your students for work?

Chapter 20

What Is Your Real Job?

Dr. Drew Bogner, president emeritus, Molloy University

Throughout your life you will be asked questions by others about who you are, common questions used to get to know others, questions that come up in polite introductory conversations. Remember when you were graduating from high school and people would ask you where you were going to college or doing in the next couple of years. If you looked "college age," people asked where you were going to college and what you were studying or what your major was. For some, the answer was easy. You knew at sixteen where you were going and what you wanted to study. For others, it was more complicated because you didn't know or you hadn't decided or committed to a path or you had some suspicion that the answer you would give wasn't what the person asking the question wanted to hear.

The good news is that after college graduation you won't have to answer those questions anymore. However, you will be asked some other defining questions for many years to come. Questions such as, "Where do you come from?" or "What do you do?" Both standard, very common questions that you will be asked thousands of times by the time you get to my age.

Let's start with the question of where you are from. For some the answer is easy because you have lived in only one place or you're from a place that people can relate to, have visited, or find intriguing. For others, the answer to the question is more complicated, because you know the follow-up dialogue that your answer might evoke.

When I came to Long Island, people could tell from my accent that I wasn't from there, and since it was perfectly acceptable in polite conversation to ask where you are from, they did. I readied myself and said, "I'm originally from Kansas," paused, and waited for a "clever" *Wizard of Oz* reference, such as,

"Did you come in on a tornado?" or "How's Toto?" or "Did you click your heels together three times?" I knew that people were just trying to relate to my experience, and since most people on the East Coast have never traveled to Kansas, the only reference they had was *The Wizard of Oz*. But now that I am living in Massachusetts, how do I answer that question today? Am I from Massachusetts, New York, or Kansas?

When you are asked what you do, people are really asking what your job is, and that is the answer they are looking for. However, answering that question will not always be or perhaps should never be that easy to answer, just as answering where you are from is not easy if many places have defined, influenced, and shaped your life.

Some jobs are easy to define, since people can relate to them through their own personal experiences;, others are more complicated and will take some additional explanation. The job of a university president is one of these. If I asked you as a college graduate to tell me what my job as a university president is, I'm not sure you would know how to answer the question.

As I got older, I would be asked if I had children and what they did. I have two. My son is co-owner of a theater booking and production company. I have found that what that all means takes some explanation. My daughter is a writer and an artist and has had several online businesses, and that is how I used to answer the question, but today I say she is an activist, because that is what she does. She has Twitter page with thousands of followers. What she does is try to change people's perspectives, educate and inspire them, and provide a forum for others to do the same. She is willing to tell the unvarnished truth, to question assumptions, and to call others to account. In doing so she has been unfriended, blocked, and called all manner of names. At times it is a fifteen-hour, seven-day-a-week job, because justice and truth can never be on holiday in a world that is so full of anger, mistrust, and deceit. She is trying to change the world, doing her part.

When I became a parent as some of you will also experience, I remember thinking that I wanted my children to learn from their earliest years that helping others is what we do, so we did toy drives and food drives together and asked our neighbors to help. We talked about what was happening and what should be done, and my wife and I voted, bringing the kids with us to the polling place and into the voting booth to pull the lever that cast our vote. Clearly something stuck.

A few years before he died, I had the honor and privilege to have lunch with congressman and civil rights activist John Lewis, who was on campus to speak with our first-year students who had just finished reading the first two volumes of his graphic novel *March*. Although he had served in the House of Representatives for more than fifteen terms and was still serving in that role and was an ordained Baptist minister, he would tell you that his real job was that of an activist who spoke the truth and advocated for justice and right action. He had put his body on the line numerous times at sit-ins, as a Freedom Rider, on marches, one of which was across the Edmund Pettus Bridge in Selma, Alabama, where he was beaten, and his skull fractured by Alabama state troopers. He decided to take these actions, noting that he had been quiet for too long and that there comes a time, he said, when you have to say something, you must make a little noise, you have to move your feet, and that was and is that time.

He told the students to never be afraid to get into "good trouble, necessary trouble." It is never too late to join the struggle because it is not a struggle of a day, or a month, or a year but the struggle of a lifetime. There is always more to do and for each generation a new struggle.

There are so many issues in the world today that cry out for attention. Surely some of these are worthy of your time and your talent. Let's say it is about ending poverty, or homelessness, or child hunger, or racism, or perhaps it is promoting diversity, or gender equality, or mentoring those who have less opportunity. Perhaps it is something of personal significance to you or something you can bring to your company's attention and ask for their support. Many companies have numerous charities and causes they support and would welcome your involvement. Find your place and cause to get into good trouble and become an activist.

So now when you are asked what you do, take that split second to pause, think about what the answer really is, and then answer in the way the question is intended. You are more than your paid job. You are a person who wants to make the world better, bit by bit. This is your real job.

QUESTIONS FOR REFLECTION

1. What is an issue in the world that you want to help solve?
2. How will you devote your time and talent to make progress on this issue?
3. How and where are you willing to get into "good trouble"?

Chapter 21

Voting Is an Act of Choice and an Exercise of Voice

Dr. Robert A. Scott, president emeritus, Adelphi University

Democracy as a functioning governing system assumes choice—informed choice—as a fundamental premise. We can choose which political party to prefer, which candidate to support, and which policy proposals to choose. However, we seem to have more safeguards on product safety than on the right to vote. Why are there so many efforts to limit access to voting?

For a country obsessed with ranking of sports teams and colleges, it is outrageous that we are satisfied with ranking #31 in voter turnout of those eligible among forty-nine other countries, according to the Pew Research Center in 2020. That's a choice too.

The 2020 presidential election campaigns spent almost $14 billion, and turnout was higher than any other in 120 years—yet one-third of eligible voters stayed away. Some were deemed ineligible by local election officials, and others lacked access or were afraid of the unofficial "marshals" monitoring voting sites. Still others didn't think their vote mattered or were dissuaded from voting by false advertising on the mainstream media and disinformation spread through social media. An irony of this is that the public airwaves used to disseminate inaccurate information are allocated by Congress, the elected representatives of the public.

Across the country, efforts are underway to curtail voters and voting and reduce the impact of citizen voices. According to the Brennan Center for Justice, twenty states have imposed new restrictions. These efforts include limiting the days and hours of voting, restricting mail-in voting, keeping even those who paid for their crimes with prison from voting, and disinformation campaigns to discourage voting and create false impressions of candidates and views. The effect is to limit who can vote, when they can vote, and how votes will be counted.

We claim to have a representative democracy but tolerate efforts to limit representativeness. What are we afraid of? Other Western democracies in Australia, Canada, and the United Kingdom have more flexible systems for voting. If we worry that Americans are not smart enough or knowledgeable enough, the answer is to strengthen the teaching of civics, U.S. history, and the meaning and methods of our Constitution. It has been called, after all, our nation's "owner's manual."

We have plenty of opportunities to practice democracy: local neighborhood elections, school board elections, fire district elections, and town, county, state, and federal elections. We need to reduce limitations to voting, control efforts at disinformation, help voters learn the truth, and ensure the integrity of elections. We can do more to ensure informed choices at the ballot box. But not choosing to do so is itself a choice, a choice that can lead to the demise of democracy.

That is what happens in authoritarian regimes, even though they may not start that way. For example, Putin was elected by popular vote first in 2000 and proceeded to institute changes in 2018 that allow him to remain in power.

The insurrection at the U.S. Capitol on January 6, 2021, resulted from a disinformation campaign that persists to this day. For democracy to survive, for there to be "a more perfect union," we need an informed citizenry that understands and appreciates critical thinking, information literacy, and the instruments of democracy. We need reliable, trustworthy, nonpartisan journalism as the source of news.

It is encouraging to learn about volunteer groups that meet and question candidates, write postcards to encourage voter registration and voting, and generate donations to civic groups that encourage support of our democracy. While news media focus on the big donations to political action committees, candidates, and parties, it has been shown over and over that many small donations build up in big ways.

We need more flexibility in voting to meet the needs of our modern world. Voting by mail, absentee ballots, and early voting are steps forward but not the only steps we could take. Why is general election voting limited to the first Tuesday in November? Wouldn't it make sense to allow voting over several days, as in some other countries? What about holding elections on a weekend, when fewer people would have to take time off from work to vote? What about requiring paid time off for voting? In some countries, voting is mandatory and fines can be imposed on those who do not vote.

Our vote is our voice. Voting is an act of choice and the exercise of our voice in expressing our values and priorities. We should make it easier to learn about candidates and issues, and for citizens to fulfill their civic duty by voting. It is intended to be a personal act for the common good.

QUESTIONS FOR REFLECTION

1. Have you registered to vote? If not, do you know how to register?
2. Why is it important for every eligible voter to vote?
3. Have you witnessed attempts to deny the right to vote? What did you do?

Chapter 22

Thinking Globally, Acting Locally

Dr. Robert A. Scott, president emeritus, Adelphi University

There has never been a better time to be in college. There has never been so much attention given to the quality of programs and the accountability of institutions. There have never been so many institutions of higher education, so many degree programs, so many nondegree opportunities. There has never been as much student aid available or so many counseling programs and flexible schedules to make college accessible to those who work and those who are the first in their family to attend.

This is also a great time to enter the job market, and it will get better. A social science sage once said that "demography is destiny." And the demographics are in your favor. The decline in the number of persons aged –eighteen to thirty, which so concerns employers, the military, and colleges alike, will be to your benefit, no matter what your age. Job offers and salaries will increase for the well prepared because of the forces of supply and demand. The supply of talented people ready to enter the workforce will decline and the demand will increase.

In fact, the next ten years will be a great time for your career search. It is estimated that one hundred thousand people retire and that about two hundred thousand jobs are created each month, just in the U.S. In the global market, opportunities multiply, amplified by global interdependence.

Increasingly, the world in which we live is interdependent. Actions by one person or group or nation can affect the circumstances of another dramatically, even if they are thousands of miles apart. We can see this in Ukraine.

Singular events with dramatic consequences have always occurred. That is not new. What is new is that the consequences can be so far reaching because of the dramatically increased interaction and interdependence of people.

Through telecommunications and jet travel, both currency and disease are spread in ways never imagined. Third world debt is not a concern limited to the big New York banks; many local banks are exposed because of questionable practices.

In simpler days, disease had time to become evident before a person could spread it beyond the local population. Now, jet travel means an infectious disease can be spread thousands of miles away from its origin even before it becomes evident to the carrier.

This increasing interdependence of people, and the greater concern about long-term and distant consequences of local actions, led Rene Dubos, the Pulitzer Prize–winning microbiologist and author, to say that the general formula of management for the future must be to "think globally and act locally."

As a scientist, Dubos understood natural systems, and how an action in one part of a system could cause consequences in another part. He then applied that reasoning to social or human systems and helped change the way we think.

This now seems obvious to us, especially after watching the ecological consequences of oil spills and forest fires. The action of one person can have a major effect on an entire ecosystem. It also has a major consequence for communities and business in this country.

Once we begin to use this "systems" approach, and appreciate how local action can have global impact, we see how it unfolds. Many scientists agree that gases resulting from industrial and other human activity are trapping heat from the sun in a process like that which happens in a greenhouse. This warms the earth's surface and affects the levels of the oceans and the climate.

Sulfur dioxide emissions from Gary, Indiana, cause acid rain damage to forests in Canada, which affects both plant and wildlife. Both treated and untreated sewage decays in water and uses up oxygen in the process. These effects should be of concern to all of us.

Biologists have studied ecology, the relationships that living things have to each other and their environments, for many decades. However, it is only in recent years that scientists and policymakers in large numbers have come to realize that the principles of interdependence that may be seen in a single forest, or an island, also apply to planet Earth and its place in space.

Rene Dubos and others helped make us realize that the same principles apply to human or social interactions. In discussing this, Dubos said, "Just as biological diversity facilitates Darwinian evolution, so is cultural diversity essential for social progress." In so doing, Dubos formulated his global-local idea.

The use of systems thinking for considering consequences both broadly and narrowly, for contemplating the consequences of interdependence among peoples and societies, is now applied to other spheres of life as well. I believe it provides a useful backdrop for talking about education, economic development, civic responsibilities, and career choices.

Think globally, act locally. Think and act—global and local. These are powerful pairs. Think! Reflect! Act, become involved! Think with the widest possible lens, to take in as much as possible, and then decide—act—take the first step, locally, today.

Ernest Boyer, former president of the Carnegie Foundation for the Advancement of Teaching, talked about education as a seamless web from nursery school through postdoctoral study. That's the global view. But how many two- and four-year colleges design articulation agreements so that the community college transfer can begin study at the four-year college with the same status as those who were sophomores the year before?

How many of us complain about the state of our schools, especially urban schools, but do nothing about it? School boards wait, PTAs wait, possible mentoring relationships wait. We cite the global problem but neglect the local action. And, just as in environmental concerns, it takes all of us acting locally to affect the global condition for good or ill.

During the past several decades, there has been a growing interest in the incorporation of global knowledge into the curriculum of schools and colleges. For some, this interest has become urgent. We know the imperatives. National security is an imperative; economic competitiveness is an imperative; environmental interdependence is an imperative; the increasing ethnic and religious diversity of our towns and schools is an imperative; the fact that many of our citizens will work for foreign-owned global firms is an imperative; the fact that even small businesses must deal with international trade, currency, and products is an imperative; the fact that our school and college graduates will likely be supervised by or will supervise persons of different ethnic and nationality groups is an imperative; and, yes, peaceful, respectful relations between nations is an imperative.

The economic reasons alone are compelling. Nearly every aspect of our economy is affected by the actions of other nations: from the price and selection of cars to the mortgage rates we pay and the foods we eat. A significant proportion of all American-made goods compete with international rivals. At the same time, 40 percent of reported profits of Fortune 500 firms are from overseas operations. For these reasons, and those cited earlier, schools and colleges must have a global perspective if we are to have a properly educated citizenry and succeed in the global economy. But this takes local action by school boards, teachers, trustees, and each of us.

Walk down the main street of any town and you will see the global impact: foods, building materials, cars, businesses closed due to global competition, new businesses opened, jobs created by foreign firms, and diversity in the population.

But look at the schools. Do our school and college curricula include readings and discussions about the history, literature, and heroes of other cultures, or of other peoples in our own culture? It takes local action to make these changes, local action in response to a global imperative.

I believe that this theme of "think globally, act locally" applies to career preparation as much as it does to concerns about the environment and an informed citizenry. Think globally: study other cultures. Act locally: study the language that will provide you with the greatest mobility. After all, it is said that we can buy in any language but can sell only when we know the language of the customer.

This thinking applies to all of us: managers, professionals, skilled tradespeople. None of us is immune. All who will live, will live in an increasingly interdependent, internationally competitive world economy. To succeed, we must be prepared by our education.

Think globally, on as grand and large a scale as you can, so that you can visualize the connections and interactions, both actual and potential. And act, exercise your knowledge, engage your mind, show your concern for education, the environment, the economy, and the freedom that undergirds them all. Act today, where you are. And just think what a world we would have if everyone would think globally and act locally.

QUESTIONS FOR REFLECTION

1. What do you think is meant by "think globally and act locally"?
2. In what ways have you and your family been affected by global forces?
3. Have you studied a language other than your native language? Have you spoken with others in that language?

Chapter 23

Acting as a Guest on the Planet

Dr. Drew Bogner, president emeritus, Molloy University

If you have ever seen the sun rise, been able to see it in its full expanse, stretching across the sky, given it your total focus, watching it as it transitions from one color in the spectrum to another, you know how really dynamic and special it is to witness and be part of this spectacle. I have seen the sun rise crimson red over Miyajima Harbor in Japan, break over the ocean from the dunes on Cape Cod, and rise above the carved red rocks of Monument Valley in the Southwest.

Watching the sun rise over Monument Valley, it occurred to me how important and necessary it is to experience the wonder of creation, to treasure the gift of life with the fullness it deserves. How lucky, blessed, and truly gifted we are to be residents of planet Earth. As cognizant, self-aware creatures, this sense of wonder and amazement is tempered or perhaps enhanced by the understanding that we are temporary residents who come into the world and eventually leave it. Somewhat like visitors who come and then go.

When a person comes to stay and visit a friend, they know that there are certain acceptable ways to act. We are polite and thankful. We certainly don't walk around touching everything, opening drawers, taking photos down from the wall, and slipping small knickknacks into our pockets to keep.

In many ways, this is what it is really like to be alive. For a person's time is limited. We come into the world and eventually we will exit it. We can own things, but only for a short time, before these possessions pass on to others or fade away. Each person, however, can choose how to live life, how to be in relation to others: humans, animals, and plants, the communities where you reside and visit, the planet, fragile and magnificent.

Standing on the beach at Poipu on the island of Kauai watching the massive green sea turtles come on to the beach, one by one, until they numbered twenty, thirty, and more, it became stubbornly clear. The turtles were coming on the sand to sleep in a space that offered protection. It was a behavior that was rare on other Hawaiian islands. People who were visiting from across the globe gathered behind orange cones, wooden stakes, and yellow caution tape, to watch in awe, talking in hushed tones. The word quickly spread across the beach and more came to watch and learn.

Some hotels along this stretch of sand also recently agreed to turn off their outside lights at the time in which newborn turtles were hatching from their eggs buried in the sand, allowing the hatchlings to find the ocean more easily.

All of this made an impression on me. We can, it seems, coexist in a thoughtful way with other living creatures if it is a priority, and because we have altered so much of the planet, find ways to protect nature and allow what still survives to thrive. The reefs that surround the Hawaiian Islands are vibrant and full of life, but these magnificent structures are also fragile and slow growing. Reefs support all manner of life. Today, even unlike a few years ago, you see many efforts to protect the reefs, for example, signs encouraging the use of reef-friendly sunblock and the use of compostable material for everything from straws to silverware to food containers, rather than the use of plastics that decompose at a glacier pace and clog beaches and waterways.

Residents and visitors seem to accept this responsibility as a necessary payment for the privilege of experiencing the wonder of it all. Not every place and not everyone around the planet accepts responsibility in this way, so it falls to us to learn and live in ways that lighten our footprint on the planet and lead by example.

It often takes cognizant, thoughtful actions, a bit like how we think and act when we are a guest in another's home, seeing and respecting boundaries, but it is more than that too. For we can also act in ways that can rebuild what has been lost, replacing native species, from the milkweed that supports monarch butterflies to replanting parts of the forests that once stood across the globe. We can resist the use of harmful chemicals and change our buying and consumption habits. We can allow nature to thrive, remembering that we share our world with other creatures, understanding the consequences of what we do and how we act.

Being a responsible and hospitable guest requires some restraint. It also takes self-awareness, identifying those behavioral clues of how to appropriately act within a new environment that is not our own. We know as guests that we cannot do and act in any way we want. Just think if we apply that mindset to our interactions with the oceans, beaches, mountains, forests, and parks we visit. Even more so to a person's backyard and the waterways where what we pour into the drain eventually collects, or what we spew into the air that people and creatures around the planet breathe.

Perhaps in Hawaii, people act differently because many see it as a special place, a tropical paradise, perhaps. But so, too, is the lawn behind the house; the park in the neighborhood; the field where we grow crops; the empty lot; the ocean, sky, and air. These are all special places, full of a diversity of life, complex and interwoven into a delicate balance.

The turtles on the beach will one day cease to exist, and so will the vibrant coral reefs if we do not learn to coexist. Perhaps it is we who are the guests in their environment, rather than the other way around. For if we are truly a highly evolved, intelligent, self-aware species, then we can adapt and learn and act as such, knowing in a profound way that what we do can leave a mark that will linger long after we are gone.

QUESTIONS FOR REFLECTION

1. Where have you been exposed to the beauty and majesty of nature?
2. What are some ways in which you could modify what you buy and consume to leave a lighter footprint on the planet?
3. How might you be a more responsible and hospitable guest within the world?

Chapter 24

Being a Pilgrim in Life, Not a Tourist

Dr. Drew Bogner, president emeritus, Molloy University

Molloy College (now Molloy University), where I served as president, is a Catholic institution founded in the tradition of Saint Dominic, formed in 1955 by the Dominican Sisters of Amityville. Several years ago, I traveled to the lands of Dominic with presidents of six other Dominican colleges. Together we visited the village and house in northern Spain where Saint Dominic was born over eight hundred years ago. We visited the cathedral where he made his vows and studied as well as the area in southern France where he preached and founded the first convent of sisters.

The trip was put together by Sister Jean Murray, the former president of Dominican University in Chicago. Every day she would remind us, this group of college presidents and spouses, that we were pilgrims on a journey, not tourists just casually seeing the sights.

The tourist just sees the surface of a place, checking off a list of sights to see.

- Eiffel Tower, check
- Coliseum, check
- At the Louvre, the Venus de Milo, check, and the Mona Lisa, check
- And oh, yes, photos and a selfie with each—check, check, check, and check

In fact, this tourist predilection is so prevalent that at the Louvre, more people stand with their backs to the Mona Lisa than face it. They are so intent on recording their presence that they barely look at the painting. They do not look into the eyes or contemplate the background or the play of light on the face.

The pilgrim, on the other hand, looks at things from the side, from the inside out, searching for the essence of the thing or the place or the moment. They stay and linger.

The pilgrim is on a journey that is open ended. There is a direction in mind at the beginning, of course, but unlike the tourist who simply wants to get from here to there, the pilgrim is open to what may be found along the way.

The pilgrim is open to revelation. What does this mean? It means that you allow a place, an item, or an experience to affect you on multiple levels. You spend time observing the details and the whole of it. You allow your mind to wander and your emotions to be affected. You look for meaning.

Recently I visited Crater Lake in Oregon. It is a lake formed in the caldera of an ancient volcano. It has no source of water other than rain and is hundreds of feet deep. Its surface is a brilliant bright blue, calm, almost placid, reflecting only the sky. Driving around the lake you can approach it from multiple angles. At each I surveyed the lake, noting the slight variations of color, the panorama of the whole, the small eddies along the shore, the rock formations that held the edge, the silhouette of clouds, and its remarkable clarity.

On another level, I thought of how the lake came to be, what it had witnessed, why it needed to be protected, and how the composition of the water had changed over time, reflecting the human alterations to the environment. I was entranced, but at one stop a mother and her teenage daughter were experiencing the lake in a very different way than me, treating it as a backdrop for social media posts. While the mother took photos with a cell phone, the younger woman posed and then posed again, never looking at the lake. They seemed every bit the tourist and perhaps not even that. The contrast was deafening.

There is much we can learn about ourselves and about the world if we allow it to speak to us, but this only happens if we pause and linger. Each of us has a natural curiosity. It is part of being human. It is what allows us to adapt to new situations. This curiosity is always just below the surface, and it is a most wonderful key that can unlock so much.

You do not need to travel to far-off lands to stimulate curiosity, experience insights and revelation. Being a pilgrim is more about mindset than location. A simple walk in the woods explains it all. A person can walk through the woods for exercise and follow the path to get from point A to point B. This has its purpose, but a person can also walk through the woods to see, hear, smell, and experience what is there; the arc of the forest canopy; the moss on the trunk of the tree; the small saplings struggling to find room to grow; spiderwebs glistening in the sunlight; the sound of wind in the pines; and perhaps, some thoughts about how these sights and sounds reflect a sense of self and purpose and how to live.

Finding a few moments to peer inside, to truly be in the presence of something outside daily life is how we find and renew ourselves. It is the journey, not the destination, where we spend most of our lives. The pilgrim knows this and by choice spends time just being in the now moment.

Why is this delineation between tourist and pilgrim so important in your life? It is because graduating from college is a time and place of the ending of one journey and the beginning of the next. It is also a time of contemplating which path among many to take in life.

Among all the choices that present themselves in college or right after, from career and job selection to where to live, one of the most fundamental is whether you take this next journey of your life as the tourist or the pilgrim.

You may travel along the surface of life, with your checklist in hand, setting milestones, and checking them off as you reach each one.

- Good-paying entry job with growth potential—check
- Stable relationship—check
- Promotion—check
- First house—check
- Great vacation—check
- Advanced degree—check

Each of these milestones is important, but the way in which you pursue them is important as well. My hope is that you will be as the pilgrim, open to possibility, open to revelation, open to the beauty and significance that each moment along the way brings. Listen to your heart as well as your head.

Each day on my trip to the lands of Dominic, Sister Jean would remind us to be pilgrims—to:

- Pay attention . . . listen . . . let go
- Live in the moment
- Have gratitude for all one sees . . .
- And for all one meets

Remember that at journey's end you have a purpose that is greater than the immediacy of everyday life—a purpose that is greater than yourself.

QUESTIONS FOR REFLECTION

1. In what ways are you a tourist or a pilgrim in life?
2. How can you allow yourself to be more open to revelation and possibility in life?

Chapter 25

Change Is the Only Constant

Dr. Robert A. Scott, president emeritus, Adelphi University

Change is the only constant. If we don't manage change, change will manage us.

Managing change requires knowledge, understanding, and continued improvements in skills, abilities, and values.

Many leading thinkers and opinion leaders have been sideswiped by change. What in the world could Ken Olsen, a pioneer in computing, have meant in 1977 when he said, "There is no reason for any individual to have a computer at home"?

And what did Thomas Edison have in mind when in 1922 he said, "The radio craze ... will die out in time"?

Can you imagine that in 1876 President Rutherford B. Hayes said, "Who would ever want to use a telephone?" Today, personal computers and smartphones are ubiquitous.

Someone I admire for his thoughtful analyses, Michael Kami, said:

> *Nothing is permanent except change....*
> *Technologies change.*
> *Societies change.*
> *Civilizations change.*
> *Lives change.*
> *Don't fight it, don't fear it, don't deny it.*
> *Embrace it, improve it, love it.*
> *Let go of the past!*
> *Move forward to new visions and a new destiny.*
> *In endings, beginnings are found.*

By this, I think Kami meant that we should honor the past but not be trapped by it. We need to understand the roots of our present condition to move forward.

CHANGE

We live in a time notable for the compression of time and an expansion of knowledge, both unprecedented in humanity. Think of transportation: from walking at three miles per hour to travel by space capsule hurtling at nearly twenty-five thousand miles per hour. Compression applies to our ability to communicate and create, as well as to destroy. From the abacus at two seconds per calculation to computing at trillions of calculations per second, we can collect and manipulate data to create information and knowledge.

However, we also have the capacity to destroy at unheard-of magnitudes. For fifty thousand years we used the bow and arrow, attacking one person at a time. Now, several nations have the potential for the instantaneous destruction of our planet by nuclear weapons.

Major changes are occurring in demographics, including the number, composition, and beliefs of populations; in economies, as they change from traditional to modern; in patterns of governing, including NGOs (nongovernmental organizations); in law and the interpretation of law; in the culture of work; and in expectations about accountability.

The explosion of human knowledge did not really change the basic behavior of the billions of people on this earth. We still exhibit the same emotions, positive and negative, of love and hate, of satisfaction and despair, of goodness and evil, as our earliest ancestors.

MANAGING CHANGE

Vietnamese Buddhist monk Thich Nhat Hanh talked about the "miracle of mindfulness." The lesson is to remember that there is only one important time, and it is now. The present moment is the only time over which we have dominion. The most important person is always the person you are with, for who knows if you will have dealings with any other person in the future.

This is a Zen way of saying, "Seize the moment." Take full advantage of the moment for yourself and for others. Ask, am I mindful of today's ideas and people, or am I waiting for tomorrow? Today is the most important time because it is here and has potential. The past is gone, and the future might not come. We must exercise our full capabilities every day.

When we seize the moment, we become leader of our own lives, author of our own script. We are continually learning, advancing our understanding, and seeking new ways of performing our work.

I am fascinated by the history of work. When we think of it, we realize that "jobs" are a relatively recent phenomenon.

In the public interest, President Franklin Delano Roosevelt created a "works" program that produced results that we rely upon today. Also, in the public interest, President Lyndon B. Johnson urged laws that codified jobs because he wanted to protect individuals. But jobs are fixed solutions to problems, and problems change. Jobs are eliminated, even as work expands, said the management scholar Peter Drucker.

Often, when I am given a suggestion or recommendation, I will say, "That's an answer; what's the question?" We need to be focused on questions if we are to manage change, whether in our personal lives, our groups, or our community. This is a major difference between education and training. Education prepares us for asking and answering questions; training often tells us where to find answers.

CONCLUSION

For us to live healthy lives in healthy organizations, we need enlightened forms of leadership. There are several key questions that our organizations need to understand and answer if both the enterprise and its crew are to grow and succeed:

1. What are the core competencies necessary to accomplish our strategy?
2. What type of organizational governance is needed—market, bureaucracy, clan, or other?
3. What culture do we need to accomplish our strategic goals?

These questions are intended to help ensure that we are empowered to manage change. One of the greatest assets for managing change is human judgment by people educated for the task. Machines can whir; data can be compiled; but so far, we humans are best at sorting data into knowledge and managing change.

QUESTIONS FOR REFLECTION

1. How do you interpret Michael Kami's quote?
2. What is a significant social or institutional change you have witnessed?
3. Have you had experience in managing change?

Chapter 26

Mentors Matter

Dr. Robert A. Scott, president emeritus, Adelphi University

What is a mentor? A mentor is not necessarily someone who meets on a regular schedule with a younger person for a long period of time. Mentors and role models can do that or be more intermittent in their relationship. They are usually a more experienced person who becomes a source of guidance and wisdom. It is someone who demonstrates care and concern so that the recipient can feel more confident about the steps to be taken. The mentor is a source of encouragement to raise aspirations, and the conduit to new networks.

Over the years, I have served as a mentor to students and colleagues at various stages in my career and theirs. For me, there were five people who qualify unquestionably as mentors, and others who vie for contention. Some were accidental mentors, and perhaps not aware of the role they were playing, and others were intentional.

The first was an antique dealer in Mount Vernon, New York, whose name I have forgotten, but whose kindness toward me at a time of stress was critically important. My mother had died; my sister and I lived in separate cities with different relatives while our father recovered from bankruptcy. After reuniting with them, I began "acting out" with some other junior high school boys who were prone to trouble.

After several incidents of harassing the shopkeeper, knocking on his door, and calling him disparaging names, he must have seen something in me I had not felt. He called me in, asked my name and about my family, and, after setting me straight about my behavior, offered to hire me to dust, move boxes, and answer the phone. I learned that he was a widely traveled, knowledgeable person who knew the history and provenance of each object. I don't recall working for him more than a few months, but his respect for me was an inspiration.

In eleventh grade, while other students were contemplating advanced education, I was uncertain of my future. Neither of my parents had attended college. One day, my tenth-grade biology teacher, Joe Leone, in whose class I had earned a rare A, had stopped me in the hallway and asked, "Bobby, why haven't you signed up for the SATs?" Why, indeed? No one had encouraged me. The guidance office, knowing my family circumstances, had urged me to apply to an inexpensive midwestern public university that didn't require the exams and was eager to enroll out-of-state students. I took the SA's, earned a scholarship to Bucknell, and the rest as they say, is history—a history whose critical "hinge" was a teacher whose class I had taken a year earlier, and who cared enough to encourage me.

As a sophomore at Bucknell, I had doubts about why I was in school and whether I could afford to stay, even with campus jobs. I decided that I should enlist in the U. S. Navy as my father had. Fortunately, my English professor and faculty advisor, Mildred Martin, talked me into rethinking my decision and urged me to see the dean about additional scholarship assistance. Together, they helped me figure out how I could stay financially and why I should stay intellectually. I still have the letter detailing the increased aid and the standards I would have to meet to maintain it. They taught me that it is okay to ask for help.

The president of Bucknell who invited me to join his team in admissions while I was finishing my navy tour was Charles Watts, whose memorial tribute I would write for our NYC club annual many years later. Dr. Watts had been a professor of English at Brown, and the language and cadence of his speeches reflected his years of study.

"Charlie," as we called him out of his hearing, was elegant in tempo as well as in voice, and brought a more liberal philosophy than his predecessors to the mission of the university and relations with the faculty. I was too junior to spend much time with him but was befriended by a senior member of his staff. He described and interpreted Charlie's thoughts, words, and actions. Charlie was a mentor, an inspiration, without even knowing it, and I repaid the compliment by writing a memorial he couldn't read.

Another mentor was James Perkins, someone I knew for about two decades. Soon after I arrived at Cornell as assistant dean for academic and student services in the College of Arts and Sciences, the dean for whom I worked was substituting for the provost and filling in for the president. So, in short order, I was helping in the president's office as well as the dean's office. Consequently, I knew the thinking of campus leaders about certain issues, even as I knew more about campus dynamics from my official perspective several levels down in the organization.

The miscues about student issues that ensued resulted in the president's resignation, which I thought was unfortunate. During his term, he had done more than almost any other campus leader in the U.S. to open access to African American students as well as to foster initiatives to reduce the time it takes to earn one's PhD. His leadership is notable also for the fact that his vice presidents all became heads of a university, an elite private school, or a major federal agency.

After leaving Cornell, Dr. Perkins's staff was protective of his privacy, so for several years it was difficult to meet with him. But eventually, I reconnected with him, and for over a decade we would meet two or three times a year to discuss life and my career. His lesson to me, "Secure your footing before you extend your reach," is one I pass on with regularity in my role as a mentor to others.

These five mentors are among the many teachers, advisors, professors, deans, supervisors, and secretaries who have offered me guidance and shared wisdom.

Over the years, I have served as a mentor to students and colleagues at various stages in my career and theirs. I think of a distinguished professor at Cornell whom I met when he was a freshman applicant and became my advisee, and a vice president at Cornell who was my student-assistant.

I think of the student on the Bucknell baseball team who was told that the hotels near the southern campuses on the spring schedule would not allow an African American to stay in them. A colleague and I stood up for him before the university president, so he got to go on the trip. The student became dean of a prominent law school, and we are still friends.

I think of other students who have been successful in careers in business, communications, theater, education, medicine, and law, as well as other fields. I even met a former student, a highly successful lawyer and federal official, who told me that something I had said years ago helped inform his professional direction and ethics. I was an accidental mentor to him.

In reviewing my role as one who has been mentored, and as a mentor myself, I realize that the relationship does not have to be formal and structured. The important elements are for each to take the other seriously, and to realize that each can learn from the other.

Think about the mentors you have known, and those you have mentored. You may have become a mentor almost accidentally for a classmate, a teammate, or someone at work or in the residence hall. Just think broadly about the purpose and value of mentoring. It does not have to be long and costly; it is about sincere and authentic relationships, valued contact, and fostering opportunities for others.

QUESTIONS FOR REFLECTION

1. Did you have a mentor or someone in your life who has acted like a mentor?
2. Have you been a mentor to another person? In what ways were you that mentor?
3. What is the difference between a mentor and an advisor?

Chapter 27

Being a Connoisseur of Knowledge

Dr. Drew Bogner, president emeritus, Molloy University

What does it mean to be educated? Does it mean that you know a lot about a little? That you have, in college, acquired a deeper understanding of a subject, or that you have prepared for a career in a particular profession, such as accounting, nursing, teaching, or engineering? Conversely, does being educated mean that you know a little about a lot? That you understand the sweep of history, have sampled literature, art, music? Does it mean that you can engage in thoughtful conversation, have a working knowledge of science, human physiology, ecology, or numerous other subjects?

Perhaps it is both, having a deep understanding of a few areas that you can apply and use, as well as a broad understanding of a variety of subjects. Most importantly, it means that you know how to sift through information to find reliable sources that provide explanatory insight and solid, reputable facts and data.

What does it mean to be educated? It means that you see the world with discerning eyes. You want to know how it works and why it is the way it is. You want to know the big picture and understand the details that contribute to the whole. You want to experience the world, expanding your horizon. Being educated means that you have made a lifelong commitment to continue to learn and become a responsible connoisseur of knowledge.

A connoisseur of knowledge understands that there are various concepts and theories that can be used to explain and make sense of most any phenomenon or part of life. They know which theory or concept or set of facts to select and apply or use in various situations. If they don't know it, in hand, they know where to go to find it. In this way a connoisseur of knowledge is just like any other connoisseur of art or music or food. They know how to categorize, organize, and select human creations, applying them in sensible and impactful ways.

A sommelier is an expert in wine. This person knows how to identify various vintages of wine, how to categorize them into regions and types, and how to pair them with various situations and food to bring out flavor and heighten enjoyment. A connoisseur of knowledge does much the same thing, knowing which concept or theory or set of facts to pair with individual situations to bring heightened awareness.

Today being educated is less about knowing facts and more about knowing concepts, theories, and organizing principles. It is also about knowing where and how to find reputable sources of information and having enough of a working knowledge of something to know what information out there is rubbish and what is more likely true and factual.

Not all information is created equal, and not all explanations or opinions are equally true and valid. In a person's professional life, this fact is widely known and ascribed to as being true, but somehow, this professional skepticism is set aside when it comes to the myriad of phenomena that impacts daily lives. An engineer or nurse or accountant wouldn't expect that they could design a building, treat a patient, or issue an audit using their own random concoction of standards and evidence. Yet many individuals don't always seek out experts or search reputable sites, relying instead on hearsay, social media, and advice from friends and acquaintances.

All accredited colleges and universities have specific educational goals and outcomes for graduates from their institutions. The general education goals, those that every graduate is expected to meet, are listed in the college catalog. Over time, these goals have changed to reflect this emphasis on educating students to become adept at finding verifiable information, a set of skills referred to as "information literacy." Many institutions emphasis the development of problem-solving skills, scientific literacy with an emphasis on the scientific method, and critical thinking skills. The general education curriculum requires history so that students understand historical analysis, art or music or literature to understand aesthetics and the foundations of culture, and courses that ask students to gain a global perspective and an understanding of diversity. All of these courses, curricula, and learning experiences are designed to help each student acquire the underpinnings necessary to become a connoisseur of knowledge.

A college education is just the start of a remarkable journey that can lead to lifelong curiosity and a desire to learn, honing those skills that were introduced in college. Like most things in life, though, it is up to everyone to make the decision whether to remain closed, rigid, and unchanging or continue to evolve, developing and expanding a person's capabilities.

After college there is still much to learn and understand. What does a connoisseur of knowledge need to know to navigate the ever-changing, complex world of being an adult in a modern, industrialized, democratic society? First, it is important to know how government works, how decisions are made. and how a person can influence these decisions at the local, state, and federal levels. It is also important to generally understand what laws and judicial decisions impact daily life, from employment law to commercial law, to liability requirements. It is also important to know the fundamentals of significant government programs from Social Security to Medicare and Medicaid and how the legal system, health care system, and educational system are structured and what rights and privileges a person has.

It is useful to have a working knowledge of economics, banking, and investments as well as an understanding of the environment, ecosystems, and weather. Since so much depends on maintaining a healthy lifestyle, it is important to understand human physiology, nutrition, and exercise, as well as basic disease processes and treatments and an understanding of genetics.

We live in a complex society, so navigating it effectively can be enhanced by a working knowledge of sociology, psychology, and cultural diversity with some sense of the major events in global history. Today it is practically impossible to live without technology, so keeping up to date seems immensely useful.

It is a long list, but each of these packets of information are like threads that together form the supporting web that holds life together in a complex society. In the final analysis, being educated means knowing how to effectively navigate and operate within the world. This is what a connoisseur of knowledge and college graduate knows and does.

QUESTIONS FOR REFLECTION

1. What do you think it means to be an educated individual in today's world?
2. Do you agree with the list of various types of knowledge that a connoisseur of knowledge needs to know for today's world, and should anything be added to the list?
3. What is a set of knowledge that you would like to acquire or expand?

Chapter 28

Being Good, Not Great

Dr. Drew Bogner, president emeritus, Molloy University

If you have ever visited the Smithsonian Institution in Washington, DC, you know that as you enter the American History Museum, you see right in front of you a stunning metal sculpture of the American flag thirty feet tall by sixty feet wide. Behind it, displayed in the dimmest of light, is the flag that flew over Fort McHenry in the War of 1812—the Star-Spangled Banner—an icon of American freedom. On summer days, crowds queue up by the hundreds to see this exhibit.

Outside this holy room, around to the left, displayed in the lobby between two hallways, is a simple lunchroom counter. Here some individuals stop and read the sign; others move on and pass by it, largely ignoring the exhibit. A few stop and engage in lively, animated conversation. This lunchroom counter is also an icon of American freedom.

Ironically, one fall, after visiting the Smithsonian, Joseph McNeil was in my office, a guest to meet the essayist Malcolm Gladwell, who had written about but never met Mr. McNeil. It was Mr. McNeil's sixth or seventh time visiting Molloy. He was a witty, pleasant, unassuming man, but he was also a hero.

We spoke about how we rightly honor those heroes of patriotism who fought in various wars. The Star-Spangled Banner is a symbol of this. But, he said, we should also find a way to honor those heroes of social justice and those individuals who, through their courage, tenacity, and self-sacrifice, made America truly a land of freedom for all. The lunchroom counter is a symbol of this.

I was struck by this observation, and I thought of those who come to and graduate from college. You see, Mr. McNeil was and is an everyday hero. His is the story of those who answered the call to right action. He didn't seek to be seen as great but to be seen as good:

- To be seen as a good person, doing the right things
- To be seen as kind, just, and fair, advocating for and doing the right thing in all situations—regardless of consequences

In 1960, Joseph McNeil was a freshman at North Carolina A&T College in Greensboro, North Carolina. It was a time of racial segregation, when many services such as train waiting rooms, bathrooms, movie seats in theaters, and even lunchroom counters were reserved only for Whites.

Throughout his first semester, Joseph McNeil, as with many college students, often stayed up late talking with his friends about lives, their futures, their dreams, and, because of the constricted reality of segregation, the prevalence of racial injustice in America. They talked not just about their personal dreams but about the need to do the right thing.

Sometime in January, the talk of doing the right thing turned into action and McNeil suggested that they stage a sit-in. On February 1, Joseph McNeil, Franklin McCain, David Richmond, and Ezell Blair walked fifteen blocks from campus to Woolworth's department store. The store sold items to both Blacks and Whites, but the lunchroom counter was reserved exclusively for Whites. They bought some items and then sat down at the counter and asked to be served. When denied service, they produced their receipts and asked why their money was good everywhere else in the store but not at the counter. When requested to leave, they refused and stayed until the lunch counter closed. The next day, they came back with fifteen other students, and on the third day, three hundred had joined in. The protest spread to other department stores in Greensboro and then across the country. By the end of February, one month later, lunchroom counters in the North were integrated, and then on July 25 in Greensboro, they were integrated as well, as Woolworth's and the other department stores changed their company policies.

Looking back, I doubt that Joseph McNeil or his friends envisioned that their simple but courageous act of protest would ignite a national response, but when they walked that February day from the campus library to Woolworth's, they did intend to do the right thing, to stand up for justice and fairness despite the consequences. They did not intend to be seen as great men but to be seen as good and fair.

Now, this is your calling, as a college graduate: you are called upon to be good, perhaps great, but certainly good. You are called:

- To be right in your actions with others
- To be respectful of all

- To see the humanness and potential in yourself and everyone you encounter
- To be compassionate
- To seek out truth
- To inform yourself about injustices in your own community and the world

You are called to be heroes in the everyday world. Every day will present you with opportunities to do the right thing, for example:

- Opportunities at work
- In a relationship
- With a stranger you encounter
- How you spend your time and whether to volunteer
- What you buy for yourself or give away to another

There will always be opportunities, almost every day, to do the right thing, to make choices that tip the scales toward justice and compassion. Remember, Joseph McNeil was still in his teens when he took that stand for justice. As a college graduate, you are called to success, to be great, perhaps, but you are also definitely called to be good. You are called, as was Joseph McNeil, to be a hero of the everyday.

QUESTIONS FOR REFLECTION

1. When have you taken a stand for justice?
2. Why did you act in that situation and not in others?
3. What opportunities in your present life call for you to take a stand?

Chapter 29

The Gift of a College Degree

Dr. Drew Bogner, president emeritus, Molloy University

Attending college was a rarity for most Americans two or three generations ago. It you were not white and male, it was even more rare. It seems so much more common today, almost expected, and not unusual. So much so that we can almost forget what a gift it is, a gift of time spent learning about yourself and about the world, honing skills, developing expertise, charting a path for the future, and becoming the person you want to be. Just think about that phrase for a moment: "becoming the person you want to be."

Less than a century ago most Americans would not have been able to wrap their head around this concept. What you would do in life was determined by where you grew up and your socioeconomic level. If you grew up on a farm, you would become a farmer; if you grew up in a mill town, you would work in the factory. A person's future was constrained by the circumstances of their birth and the level of education they had the privilege to receive.

They did not have the opportunity to go away to college for four years, living in another part of the country, perhaps even studying abroad and not having to work full-time right after high school. The whole collegiate world would have seemed out of reach and inconceivable to spend so much time learning and growing, postponing the rigor of full-time employment. It is a gift to be a college graduate—indeed, they would have seen it that way.

The vast array of colleges and universities that have been built, all those thousands of institutions that dot the American landscape, is a truly unique American phenomenon. In almost every other country you cannot choose to go to college, for there are very few open access colleges. Instead, a person is placed into technical schools or universities based on placement exam scores and preparatory school grades. The idea of personal transformation and growth, of exploration and social maturation, as a purpose for going to college is most unusual and very American. It is true that we place a high premium on the importance of college education in preparing one for a profession or a career or employment, but there is a high degree of latitude given to this journey to find oneself.

This complete journey comes at a considerable expense. At the time of writing, the actual cost of delivering a college degree at a public university is a little over $14,000. This does not include the cost of room and board since not every student lives on campus. True, the individual who is attending the institution pays for lot of it, but the government pays for part of the cost of delivering the education, providing a discount to state residents or providing student aid. Private colleges provide a significant amount of scholarships and grants that discount the actual cost to many students. For example, in New York, it amounted to $6 billion in 2020. A significant chunk of these scholarship and grant dollars comes from the largess of donors, who see the importance of a college education and want to help others to attain it. Parents and grandparents pay for a portion of the tuition, and students pay for part of it as well and go into debt, sacrificing future dollars to pay for their collegiate years.

As president of a college, I built ten buildings and as provost at another college oversaw the construction of four buildings. These were all built with tens of millions of dollars from generous donors who each, in their own way, believed in the power of education to transform individual student lives and through them to bolster, support, and transform society.

Understanding this is important, because a college degree is still a rarity, a gift, an investment you made, and others made in you. Did you ever stop to think about why we built this whole unique system of American higher education, why we spend taxpayer dollars on it, why donors invest in it, why parents pay for part of it, why a person invests four or five years in it, and why many go into debt to finance it?

The most common answer given by students or parents to the question of why invest in a college degree would be to get a job, not just any job, but one that will propel a person into a career that is meaningful and that allows one to achieve a certain lifestyle. This is all true, but it is a very narrow and highly individualistic reason for going to college and does not explain why governments, donors, and various sponsors would invest in colleges and universities and in college graduates,

The overarching reason for this investment in higher education is because of the belief that a knowledgeable and active citizenry is fundamentally important to enlivening communities; to reimagining and building and rebuilding society, the nation, and the world; to pushing out the boundaries of human existence; and to solving the issues and problems that arise in an interdependent and complex world.

Whether you knew or not, that degree that was handed to you onstage by me or another college official at graduation is an agreement, a promise, and a commitment you have made to be an active, contributing citizen who will make a difference in the lives of others. Let's take a moment to acknowledge that agreement and see what you are bound to do—the commitment I would hope you will honor.

First, you will commit to learn, to pay attention to what is happening in the world and how it is affecting not just you but others. Your horizon, your sphere of responsibility is much bigger than yourself and your family. It is your community and your profession.

Hopefully, we taught you how to be aware and how and where to find out what is really happening and how to check your sources of information so that it comes not just from conversations with friends or from social media, but from reputable places like the ones you were expected to cite in your college papers and presentations. Life is a very busy place, and you will find that you need to make learning and being aware a priority. You will need to schedule time to do this. Many professions and jobs expect that you will do this, but as an educated citizen, you will benefit the nation and your local community as well.

The second part of the compact is to commit to giving back, to paying forward the gift you were given. This can happen in several ways. First, I would like to suggest, that you choose one or two (or more) causes that you will actively support with your time, your treasure, and your talents. All are precious gifts. As a college graduate you honed and developed a set of powerful skills and abilities that can be useful to nonprofits and various charities and activist causes. You know how to communicate, make presentations, research, plan and manage projects, be a team member and a leader, just to name a few.

The capstone of the MBA program at Molloy required that a group of five students form a consulting team for a nonprofit or government agency to study and recommend action on a specific problem or issue. Their clients were always impressed by the thoroughness and skills of the students, and invariably some of these students continued to work with the agency, some even going onto their boards. Many entities that have important missions and do important work are desperate for the expertise and involvement of concerned and motivated individuals.

The third part of the compact is to be an active engaged citizen who regularly casts an informed ballot. Thomas Jefferson, the author of the Declaration of Independence and the third president of the United States, was a passionate advocate for free public education. True, he only advocated for free education for white boys, but it was still a radical idea at the time to expect a state to provide multiple years of education to each boy regardless of their station. For Jefferson believed that the surest and only way to safeguard the fledgling democracy that was the United States was to place its control within the hands of an educated populace that would make rational decisions.

As a college graduate, you are just the sort of educated citizen that Jefferson saw as the bulwark of democracy that would be involved in helping to shape and reshape the republic. Jefferson felt so strongly about the importance of a college education that he founded the University of Virginia, the first public university in America. He knew that it was not just the casting of ballots that made the difference, but the casting of ballots by those who considered this the most important of actions within a democracy. You might see this as a very small ask, but only around 60 percent or less of eligible American voters cast a ballot in the year of a presidential election. In the midterms, the average is only 50 percent.

At local elections for school boards, the number is below 40 percent. During a recent mayoral election in New York City, less than 25 percent of the electorate voted. Among voters aged eighteen to twenty-four, it is historically much lower. So, if you pledge to do this task you will be only one of the four in ten who in your age group make the commitment to cast a ballot and impact the election. Keep in mind that in today's elections you are not only voting for candidates for office but often for specific legislation that has been placed on the ballot as a referendum, so you are helping to make laws and policies.

Every time I cast a ballot, I remind myself that for almost all of us there was a time in American history when because of the color of our skin, our gender, or our economic or citizenship status we would not have been eligible to vote. The right to vote is a hard-won victory for most of us and needs to be cherished, protected, and used.

Remember as well that you were given the gift of education, a degree that wouldn't have been possible seventy-five years ago for most of you because of the same barriers: your race, your gender, your religion, or your social class. Many others who came before you fought the battles to open higher education to diversity and provide opportunity to so many more Americans.

When you have that diploma in your hand or when you hang it on the wall, remember how precious this gift is you have been given. When you see it hanging there behind your desk, ask yourself whether you are doing your part to pay it forward by being an active citizen, by serving your community, and by helping others to achieve their full potential.

My father was the first in his family to attend and graduate from high school. It was his dream to attend and graduate from college. He took a couple of night classes, but World War II intervened, and as an engineer he was called away to run modification sites for Boeing. He never made it back to college, but he took and passed the professional mechanical engineering exam using only the wealth of experience he had accumulated. I can hear him to this day saying to me, "To whom much is given much is expected."

I have, over my life, really taken this exhortation to heart. So, I say to all college graduates, "To whom much is given much is expected." This is the compact you have agreed to by accepting a college degree.

QUESTIONS FOR REFLECTION

1. How will you make a commitment to continue learning?
2. What cause(s) will you choose to commit your time, talents and treasure to?
3. How will you be an engaged citizen?

Chapter 30

Navigating the Passage through College

Dr. Robert A. Scott, president emeritus, Adelphi University

A passage is both a way of exit and of entrance. It denotes the passing from one place, stage, or condition to another. It is an apt metaphor for describing the path of first-generation students to college and the navigational tools they need to achieve success.

For all students, the passage from high school, or work, to college can be formidable. For the one-third of students who are the first in their families to enroll in college, the passage can be particularly challenging. For all students, the path is an individual one.

While first-generation students have some advantages over other students, such as greater work experience, strong motivation, and more responsibility out of the home, they also have distinct challenges. Most first-generation students attend college part-time and work also. Nearly one-third have dependents while in college.

A college or university campus is a community with rules and regulations as well as opportunities and challenges. Students, especially first-generation students, need help in navigating the varied passages from entrance to success. First-generation students are less likely to have parental or sibling guidance on admissions, financial aid, course selection, and degree requirements. Having parents who attended college increases a student's likelihood of graduating from 20 percent to 60 percent. Family members are navigational aids.

Therefore, students need to learn how to navigate institutional systems such as degree requirements, course selection, changing an advisor, and so forth. All colleges have their local lore and language: What is an RA? What is SGA? What is gen ed? When it comes to college, most first-generation students don't know what they don't know.

An important subset of first-generation students consists of those who are Black, Hispanic, and other people of color. They often do not find role models among the faculty and staff and may be identified as participants in "opportunity" programs. They face special challenges and will seek students in similar circumstances for mutual assistance. This is natural and should not be resisted.

Among the skills all students need is time management. This is particularly important skill for first-generation students as most work at least part-time in addition to their studies. Time management is critical in the first semester of college. This is when a student's reputation can be set and when confidence can be strengthened or diminished. It also is before networks of assistance are established.

To improve time management, students need to know about academic requirements and both academic and nonacademic opportunities available, then assess the time commitments they require. Guidance about which should be explored in the first year and which should be saved for a later year is essential.

Colleges abandoned in loco parentis, that is, acting as parents, long ago, and for good reason. They wanted to treat students as adults and wanted students to act as adults. In recent years, the phenomenon of the "helicopter" parent has become commonplace on campuses, as have increased health services in response to the physical and emotional needs that students bring. Students need to be advised about the availability of these services.

Navigating campus passages can be challenging. Academic degree regulations, distribution requirements, and study abroad and internship opportunities must be learned. As obvious as it may seem, students need to master how to learn, especially with no familial figure to ask, "What did you learn today?" or "What questions did you ask today?"

If the college offers a pre-entry orientation, either on campus or off, students should register for it, if possible. Many cannot because of jobs. However, these programs provide occasions to meet fellow students, professors, and staff in a relaxed setting. "Hall" meetings for those living on campus do the same. For those who commute from off campus, it is helpful to find a place in the cafeteria to hang out with others.

First-generation students should embrace their identity and reach out to schoolmates, instead of shyly staying on the sidelines. It is better to seek help and find a mentor than to try to cope on one's own.

In addition to academics, there is the student social scene. Is joining a fraternity or sorority a good idea? What about trying out for a sports team?

In both cases, students become known by and get to know adults who can be good role models and helpful allies as well as other students.

Campus jobs can provide introductions to adults who value education and who will support student success. While they take time, they can provide beneficial relationships as well as money. Some jobs also reinforce learning goals and provide extra time for reading or lab research, such as those at the library's reserve reading desk or in biology. These should be given preference over those without these benefits.

Many campuses provide chaplain services as well as counseling. Chaplains can play an important role in helping students navigate requirements and opportunities. Many provide interfaith services, which can be good ways to meet other students in small groups.

The first year Seminar provides a venue for new students, especially first-generation students, to gain a good footing with professors, librarians, student services staff, and fellow students.

The most logical sources of support for new students are the faculty members with whom they are studying. Most faculty became teachers because they love learning and were nurtured when they were students. Most will respond positively to students who want to learn about them as people.

While many of these ideas relate to students who are of traditional college age (eighteen to twenty-two), the advice applies to all. Take initiative and ask for help. It is when students remain silent, especially when facing difficult choices, that they can fall behind and let a slow start become a stalled start. Even skilled navigators need assistance to guide their passage to the desired destination.

QUESTIONS FOR REFLECTION

1. What do you think are the major barriers to academic success?
2. Who have you found to be most helpful in navigating the passage to college and beyond?
3. Have you had the opportunity to help other students become oriented to college?

About the Authors

For nearly sixteen years, Dr. Bogner and Dr. Scott served as presidents at competing universities located within five miles of each other on Long Island, New York. As student-centered presidents, they found that they shared a common concern for the holistic development of the student and a belief that a college education transforms individuals, preparing them to be active, successful citizens who achieve success and make a difference in communities.

Dr. Drew Bogner is president emeritus and professor of education at Molloy University, where he served as president for twenty years. Prior to Molloy, Drew served as executive vice president for academic affairs at Newman University. After his retirement from Molloy, he served as the interim president of CICU (Commission on Independent Colleges & Universities), the advocacy group for private higher education in New York. Dr. Bogner holds a PhD in foundations of education from the University of Kansas and teaches courses in diversity, equity, and inclusion in the EdD program at Molloy. He has previously served in numerous leadership roles with the NCAA including the executive committee.

Dr. Robert A. Scott is president emeritus and university professor emeritus of Adelphi University, where he served from July 2000 to July 2015. He also is president emeritus and professor emeritus of Ramapo College of New Jersey, where he served from 1985 to 2000. He is the only American to serve in the three top posts in higher education: head of an independent university (Adelphi); head of a public institution (Ramapo College), and leader of a state higher education coordinating agency (New Jersey and Indiana). He earned his BA at Bucknell University and his PhD at Cornell University.

Dr. Scott is an expert on governance and has experience in nonprofit, for-profit, and government organizations. He advises public and private university and nonprofit organization boards and presidents on issues of governance, leadership, strategy, community engagement, assessment, risk, and succession planning. He has conducted retreats and professional development sessions for boards and organizational leaders as well as for corporate leaders, law firms, a federal Ministry on Education, and the New England Commission on Higher Education. He has advised the State of Hawaii on consolidating disparate campuses into a state system and the Middle States Commission on Higher Education on accreditation issues. He serves as senior advisor to Grant Thornton's higher education and nonprofit practice areas and is senior consultant with AGB Consulting.

www.ingramcontent.com/pod-product-compliance
Lightning Source LLC
Chambersburg PA
CBHW030828230426
43667CB00008B/1426